Velvet Glove, **IRON FIST**

And 101 Other Dimensions of Leadership

Velvet Glove,
IRON FIST

And 101 Other Dimensions of Leadership

By
Konosuke Matsushita

PHP Institute, Inc.

Tokyo, Kyoto, New York and Singapore

This book is originally published in Japanese
by PHP Institute, Inc. under the title of
Shidosha no joken—Jinshin no myomi ni omou
(Prerequisites of Leadership: The Secrets of Charisma) in 1975

•

Published by PHP Institute, Inc.
Tokyo Head Office: 3-10, Sanbancho,
Chiyoda-ku, Tokyo 102 Japan
Kyoto Head Office: 11 Kitanouchicho, Nishikujo,
Minami-ku, Kyoto 601 Japan
Distributed in North America and Europe by
PHP Institute of America, Inc. 420 Lexington Avenue
Suite 646, New York, New York 10170 U.S.A., and
in Asia and Oceania by PHP International (S) Pte., Ltd.,
20 Cecil Street, #15-07 the Exchange,
Singapore 0104, The Republic of Singapore;
and in Japan by PHP Institute, Inc.

•

•

Printed in Japan by Tosho Printing Co., Ltd.
Cover design by Michael Gilmore

•

First Edition, July 1991
Second Printing, April 1994

Contents

Preface———ix
Note———xi

1. Velvet Glove, Iron Fist ——— 2
2. Saying What Has to Be Said ——— 4
3. Positive Anger ——— 6
4. Respect Your Enemies ——— 8
5. Dedicate Your Life ——— 10
6. The Impulse to Pray ——— 12
7. Explain Yourself ——— 14
8. Quality Not Quantity ——— 16
9. Ready to Risk Everything ——— 18
10. Don't Panic ——— 20

11. Playing Fair ——— 22
12. You Can't Fight Human Nature ——— 24
13. Listening to Criticism ——— 26
14. Give Thanks ——— 28
15. Gut Feelings ——— 30
16. Turn Higher Powers to Your Own Advantage ——— 32
17. Demand the best ——— 34
18. Keep Your Resolve ——— 36
19. Be Bold ——— 38

20. Who's to Blame? ——— 40

21. Be Humble ——— 42
22. Allocating Responsibility ——— 44
23. Knowing What Comes Next ——— 46
24. One Law for All ——— 48
25. The Need for Integrity ——— 50
26. Be Ambitious ——— 52
27. Never Switch Off ——— 54
28. Overconfidence ——— 56
29. Never Give Up ——— 58
30. Fostering Independence ——— 60

31. See Things for What They Are ——— 62
32. Believe in Something ——— 64
33. Know Your Limitations ——— 66
34. A Sense of Mission ——— 68
35. Self-Interrogation ——— 70
36. Be Ready to Listen ——— 72
37. Know When to Back Down ——— 74
38. Attention to Detail ——— 76
39. Look After Those Who Serve You ——— 78
40. Even-Handedness ——— 80

41. Leave Nothing to Chance ——— 82
42. Exercising Restraint ——— 84
43. Winning Trust ——— 86
44. Believe in Your Staff ——— 88
45. Love What You Do ——— 90
46. Everyone Has a Role to Play ——— 92
47. A Matter of Principle ——— 94
48. The Ultimate Sacrifice ——— 96
49. Vox Populi ——— 98
50. The Power of Persuasion ——— 100

51. Going Against the Flow —— *102*
52. In Touch with Tomorrow —— *104*
53. Stay One Step Ahead —— *106*
54. Don't Delay —— *108*
55. Practice What You Preach —— *110*
56. Fight for the Right Reasons —— *112*
57. The Big Picture —— *114*
58. At the Heart of Things —— *116*
59. Calling the Shots —— *118*
60. The Greater Good —— *120*

61. Do What You Know to Be Right —— *122*
62. Something in Reserve —— *124*
63. The Human Factor —— *126*
64. Who Chooses Who? —— *128*
65. The Right Man for the Job —— *130*
66. Study Your Rivals —— *132*
67. Common Property —— *134*
68. When It Rains, Use an Umbrella —— *136*
69. A Sense of Destiny —— *138*
70. An Alternative to Force —— *140*

71. Self-Reliance —— *142*
72. Keep an Open Mind —— *144*
73. Work at It —— *146*
74. Look to the Long-Term —— *148*
75. Staying on Course —— *150*
76. Put People First —— *152*
77. Empathy —— *154*
78. All Fired Up —— *156*
79. The Aura of Authority —— *158*
80. Balancing Act —— *160*

81. Strict Regimens —— *162*
82. True Education —— *164*

83. The Key to Greatness —— *166*
84. Tailor Your Approach —— *168*
85. Putting Together a Team —— *170*
86. Every Day Is a New Beginning —— *172*
87. Look Around You —— *174*
88. Nothing Is Impossible —— *176*
89. Give a Clear Lead —— *178*
90. Generosity of Spirit —— *180*

91. Credit Where Credit Is Due —— *182*
92. Delegating Responsibility —— *184*
93. Lateral Thinking —— *186*
94. Summoning Up Courage —— *188*
95. Don't Use Force Unless Necessary —— *190*
96. The Art of Issuing Orders —— *192*
97. Setting Goals —— *194*
98. Doing It Your Way —— *196*
99. Be Brave —— *198*
100. Keep Your Wits About You —— *200*

101. Beyond Reason —— *202*
102. Another Look at Modesty and
     Humility —— *204*

Index of Personal Names——*207*
Chronology of Japanese History——*210*

Preface

SOME YEARS AGO I watched a television drama series
about the life of Uesugi Kenshin, a prominent six-
teenth-century Japanese lord. One episode made a
strong impression on me. It showed what happened
after Kenshin's father was succeeded as ruler of Echigo
province by his eldest son, Harukage. The father had
ruled Echigo with a firm hand, but under the ineffectual
Harukage the province quickly lapsed into chaos. As I
watched this illustration of the way a change at the top
can utterly transform a situation, I realized just how
important a leader is.

This is no less true today, and is borne out by events
we can see for ourselves. Just as a province will flourish
under a good leader, but succumb to chaos and ruin
under a bad one, a company's fortunes depend on its
managers. Within a given company, the performance of
each division or section depends entirely on the caliber
of its management.

In the final analysis, the successful operation—or
otherwise—of any organization can be said to depend,
in a critical sense, on the person in charge.

Regardless of the size of the organization, the individual in a position of leadership must be fully aware of
the responsibility he bears, and must ceaselessly exam-

ine his own behavior and search his own heart. I bear these things in mind constantly.

To help me monitor and improve myself, I decided to study the deeds of outstanding leaders of ancient and modern times. In this way, I learned a great many truths. Finally, I selected 102 anecdotes, which I interwove with a few of my own ideas, to make this book. I regard it as a textbook for my own use: my "book to live by."

But I hope it will be read by leaders the world over, from those who hold the reins of government to those managing corporations, as well as those who will be leaders in the future. I believe that, just as I did, you will find there is much to draw from the exploits of the great leaders of the past. If you practice what you have learned, you will help your nation to develop, and also aid the progress of all sorts of organizations and enterprises. In doing so, you add to the sum total of human happiness.

In researching this book, I consulted a large number of works. I would like to acknowledge my indebtedness to the authors in question.

KONOSUKE MATSUSHITA
November 1975

Note

To sustain the flow of the text, biographical dates are included in the index. A chronology of Japanese history can be found on page 210.

Chinese and Japanese terms have been romanized in accordance with the pinyin and Hepburn systems respectively. Chinese and Japanese names are given on first reference in the traditional way, with the family name first. For Japanese names, persons from the premodern era (that is, from before the Meiji Restoration of 1868) will then generally be referred to by their given names, while post-Meiji Restoration individuals will generally be referred to by their family names. Thus Tokugawa Ieyasu will be referred to as "Ieyasu" while Katsu Kaishu will be referred to as "Katsu."

Velvet Glove, **IRON FIST**

And 101 Other Dimensions of Leadership

1

Velvet Glove, Iron Fist

A leader must strike a balance between severity and leniency

THE FOLLOWING QUOTATION IS attributed to Ikeda Mitsu-masa, one of the most famous lords of the early Edo period.

"To govern a state well, a leader must be author-itative and kind. If you never exert your authority and are always kind, then, just as spoilt children will not learn their lessons, so your subordinates will not do well. If, however, you constantly exert your authority and are always harsh, you may be successful for a while; but in the long run things will not work out because those under your command will never feel comfortable with you.

"To have real authority is to treat your subordinates kindly, and to make them feel comfortable with you, but to exercise justice so that laws are always respected.

If you are never lenient, your authority will lose its force, and if you are never severe, your kindness will become ineffective. The important thing is to familiarize yourself with the life of the common people. Unless you know how they live, you will not be capable of authority or leniency."

* * *

This is a very wise saying. Severity and leniency equate with harshness and kindness, or blame and praise. Both are needed, but they must be properly balanced. If you are always praising your subordinates, they will become complacent, and will not develop.

Conversely, if you are always scolding your subordinates, they will be reluctant to approach you with new ideas, and tend to work more and more independently, while making a show of obeying your orders. It is important not to lean too far in either direction, but to balance kindness and severity.

This does not mean that the balance should be fifty–fifty. Severity should be used much less than kindness. This allows you to be lenient, but still get the best out of people. In practice, there are some leaders who can be nice to their subordinates all the time and still get them to work hard and produce good results. This type keeps his severity well under the surface, but somehow manages to make his subordinates fully aware that he has an iron fist in a velvet glove.

As Ikeda Mitsumasa said, you become able to do this by "finding out how the common people live," or discovering what makes people tick. As a leader, the most important thing is to be careful to use severity as little as possible, and to maintain the right balance between severity and leniency.

2

Saying What Has to Be Said

A leader has to talk tough at times

PRO-IMPERIAL FORCES LED by Omura Masujiro of the Choshu domain were doing battle with forces fighting for the Tokugawa shogunate at the time of the Meiji Restoration. Omura's forces were vastly outnumbered, and when the battle began, the shogunate armies gained the upper hand and the pro-imperial forces were hard pressed. But Omura, despite his cautious nature, decided to push ahead with the battle anyway.

The fighting was particularly fierce at Kuromonguchi, where the attacking pro-imperial forces, drawn mainly from the Satsuma domain, were in danger of being overwhelmed by the defenders. When the Satsuma commander asked Omura for much needed reinforcements to press home his attack, Omura refused. The commander protested angrily. "Are you saying that the whole Satsuma army is going to be left on its own to perish here?" he asked. "Yes," Omura replied. "That is precisely the case." Upon hearing this, the Satsuma troops, realizing they were doomed otherwise, charged with all their might and won the battle.

On another occasion, Omura's allies hesitated to ford a river, and the general turned on them, shouting and herding them into the water. Once wet, the force went on to win a great victory.

* * *

Omura Masujiro used harsh words in harsh situations. If he had told the Satsuma commander that there was nothing to be worried about, the army's desperate charge might never have happened and victory would have eluded it. Omura Masujiro was a great commander and brilliant tactician: in the battles of the Meiji Restoration, his forces won through by virtue of his quick grasp of military essentials and his ability to issue harsh commands when necessary.

These incidents took place in war, but in any circumstances a leader must be strong enough to say what needs to be said. A leader who fails in this may win short-term popularity by flattering those under his command, but he ends up by making his subordinates careless. He must always find within himself the strength to say what needs to be said and elicit from others what they are truly capable of achieving.

3

Positive Anger

A leader must lose his temper when necessary

WHEN WEST GERMAN CHANCELLOR Konrad Adenauer met U.S. President Dwight Eisenhower, he is said to have remarked that a man begins to understand life only after he reaches seventy years of age, but that no matter how old he gets, he should not forget how to get angry.

*   *   *

Having a temper and being prone to lose it is usually considered a sign of weakness. We admire those who keep their temper in check and maintain harmonious relations with everyone.

But Adenauer is referring not to personal feelings or spite, rather to anger based on a moral imperative —

positive anger, or anger for the public good. While it is certainly undesirable for a leader to lose his temper for personal reasons, a leader must be able to express anger when the situation warrants it.

Adenauer took West Germany in hand after the devastation of World War II, and helped build it into one of the world's most prosperous nations. He was able to do this because, as chancellor of West Germany he turned his powerful anger on things that went against the interests of his nation.

The leader of a nation must be able to use his anger for the good of his people. The head of a company must be able to guard his temper, but use it when necessary, or he will be incapable of strong management. When the world faces difficult times, a leader must avoid being swayed by personal feelings and confront the situation with virtuous anger.

4

Respect Your Enemies

A leader must be impartial

UESUGI KENSHIN AND TAKEDA Shingen were arch rivals who fought many fierce battles. Shingen's territory was a mountainous region far from the sea. On one occasion, after he had quarreled with neighboring lords, they cut off supplies of salt to his territory and his people suffered.

When Kenshin heard this, he sent a letter to Shingen. "I hear that your salt supplies have been cut off," he wrote. "This is a cowardly way for military commanders to behave. Victory or defeat should be decided on the battlefield, so I shall send you as much salt as you need." Good as his word, Kenshin then sent salt and Shingen and his followers were duly grateful for his largesse.

* * *

Uesugi Kenshin was renowned for his courage and is said to have fought like a demon in battle, but he also had a strong sense of honor and compassion. He was a thoroughly well-rounded commander, and this is why he has had many admirers throughout history.

Usually one is supposed to rejoice at an enemy's suffering. Indeed, many people would seize the opportunity to attack. Kenshin, however, thought differently. He fought for the sake of military honor, not for the chance to cause general unhappiness. When Takeda Shingen's subjects were suffering from the salt embargo, he saw it as his duty to redress the balance by providing salt to his enemies, even though he might later meet them on the battlefield.

Competition and rivalry are found everywhere today: between countries, between political parties, between corporations, and between groups. Sometimes, this competition descends to the level of sheer spite, resulting in a hard-fought, bitter campaign that only serves to make things miserable for all concerned. Competition is a necessary facet of life, and rivalry is not always bad. But a leader should try to be impartial and generous enough to respect his enemies, just as Uesugi Kenshin was.

5

Dedicate Your Life

A leader must have the strength of purpose to dedicate his life to the task at hand

---

EARLY IN THE DISTINGUISHED diplomatic career of Komura Jutaro, he was charged with resolving a dispute between Japan and Korea. Feeling quite unequal to the task of handling such a prominent international issue, Komura visited elder statesman Katsu Kaishu to seek his advice.

"I myself experienced great difficulty when dealing with important negotiations," said Katsu, "but I came to the conclusion that if you concern yourself with your own survival, you can't really do your job properly. Only when you commit yourself without reservation to giving your life for your country can you clearly see all the possibilities open to you." On hearing this, Komura was greatly encouraged, and was able to devise a successful strategy.

*　　*　　*

"Dedicating your life" is a common enough expression, but Katsu Kaishu applied it quite literally and to great effect, brilliantly handling many crises at the time of the Meiji Restoration.

Only when you are fully prepared to commit yourself to something can you begin to summon up the courage to overcome any adversity. Most of us, of course, find it very difficult to deal calmly with the thought of actually sacrificing our lives. But think about it in a different way. Every time we walk down the street or get in a car, we are putting ourselves at mortal risk.

Follow this logic and it is not a difficult thing to dedicate your life to an issue that is really important to you. Any leader must think this way to some extent.

6

The Impulse to Pray

*A leader should have
the humility to seek
divine assistance*

MATSUDAIRA SADANOBU, COUNCILOR TO the Tokugawa shogun, is said to have made the following prayer: "I earnestly entreat, even at the price of my own life and the lives of my wife and children, that this year's rice harvest will be good, that the price will not rise too high, and that the people will be free from distress and live in peace. If this prayer is not answered and the people suffer, then I beg to be struck dead on the spot."

According to his autobiography, he also bowed several times a day in the direction of Toshogu Shrine — the burial place of Tokugawa Ieyasu, the first Tokugawa shogun — asking for the strength to carry out his heavy responsibilities.

The years before Sadanobu came to power were plagued by disasters and financial chaos: governments were corrupt, law and order broke down, and prices spiralled. In order to bring matters under control, Sadanobu developed a plan for radical government reform. He was sufficiently devoted to it to offer his own life to achieve it. His humility and sincerity enabled him to achieve some extraordinary results, and he became one of the great men of the late Tokugawa period. The prosperity of those times is generally attributed to his skills.

*   *   *

As human beings, we have to accept that there are moments when we are powerless and must seek divine aid. We must also accept that such aid may not arrive exactly in the manner that we hope or expect.

When someone is genuinely sincere about achieving a goal, however, vowing to succeed at all costs, the impulse to pray arises as a matter of course. This may be in the form of an explicit prayer or simply as a fervent hope that things will work out in the desired manner. Either way, this helps to express earnestness and determination, and is something to cultivate.

A leader's prayer should not be merely for himself but, like Matsudaira Sadanobu's prayer, for his people and for the general good. Therein lies the priceless value of such a prayer.

It is important for a leader to approach all matters with true sincerity, and to ask himself, when faced with a problem, whether or not he is able to offer up a prayer.

7

Explain Yourself

A leader must always make his intentions clear to those around him

---

SANADA YUKIHIRO INHERITED THE Matsushiro domain at the age of thirteen. When he came of age three years later, the domain's finances were heavily strained and he assigned the task of fiscal reform to one of his youngest councilors, Onda Moku.

Onda Moku first summoned his relatives to his residence. "Today," he said, "I have assumed a heavy responsibility, and I must take it upon myself to lead a life of extreme frugality from now on. But I cannot impose this hardship on my family. I shall now divorce my wife, disinherit my sons, and disown my relatives so that I can carry out this task." When they heard this, all were aghast. "No!" they pleaded with him. "We will do whatever you ask of us! Do not disown us!" Onda Moku was happy at this response.

Next, he summoned his most influential subjects, and, in the presence of domain officials, requested their cooperation in the reforms. He asked these leading citizens to accept a temporary suspension of the domain's outstanding debts until the financial situation had stabilized. In return, he said, the domain would run public finances on a normal basis and refrain from levying ridiculously high taxes. The citizens saw that Onda Moku was going about things in a fair and sincere way. This won their trust, and they agreed to the debt suspension so that domain finances could be restored. This had the effect of uniting the government and the people, and Onda Moku's reforms were highly successful.

*　*　*

As a leader, when you want to achieve something, it is vital to explain your intentions to those under you. Whether you are leading a nation or a corporation, you must let people know exactly which way you are heading, and exactly what demands you are going to make of them. Making your intentions clear is important in any situation, but it is essential when you are faced with a major difficulty or emergency. In this situation, it is natural to hesitate and wonder what to do. But a strong relationship between a leader and his people will develop the spirit to enable them to overcome any adversity.

To do this, of course, you must have the courage of your convictions and stand firm. As a leader, you must develop this courage within yourself.

8

Quality Not Quantity

---

*A leader must learn
to judge the proper value
of things*

TODO TAKATORA WAS AN exceptional man who rose from
humble beginnings to a position of great power. He
came to the attention of Toyotomi Hideyoshi, and was
later given high rank by Tokugawa Ieyasu. As well as
being awarded a substantial fief in Ise, he was the only
non-Tokugawa lord to play an important advisory role
in the government of the early Tokugawa shogunate.

One day, Takatora hired a famous samurai, Watanabe Satoru, paying him the unusually high stipend
of 20,000 *koku* [samurai income was computed in terms
of rice yields with one *koku* equivalent to five U.S.
bushels]. When he heard this, another lord laughed
at Todo. "However strong Watanabe Satoru may be,"
he said, "he could always be overpowered by a gang
of men. It's a waste to give 20,000 *koku* to one man.

If I were you, I would engage a hundred samurai at 200 *koku* each."

"Not so," Takatora replied. "If I were to gather a hundred, even two hundred obscure samurai about me, my enemies could still crush them. But if they hear that I am protected by the famous Watanabe Satoru, most of my enemies will be too frightened to attack. His value is beyond compare." Sure enough, in many battles thereafter, Takatora's side achieved victory thanks to the presence of Watanabe Satoru.

* * *

Todo Takatora understood the value of things. It is true that on a superficial level, the argument put forward by the other lord seems reasonable. But Watanabe Satoru's courage was known far and wide and this had its own intangible value. Takatora rated this intangible value so highly that he did not begrudge paying highly for the warrior's services.

Everyone needs to be able to judge the correct value of things, but for a leader this skill is absolutely indispensable. In any company, there will be some personnel who are not worth a salary of ¥100,000 per month, and some who would be cheap at ¥1 million per month. If you are unable to assess the value of your staff, you will be equally unable to make full use of them. Moreover, unless you understand your company's management, technical, and financial strengths, you will end up making mistakes in business. In the same way, those who manage a nation must base their policies on a correct awareness of the country's history, traditional values, and overall national strength. It is extremely important that a leader be able to make such value judgments.

9

Ready to Risk Everything

A leader must be resolute in a crisis

SASAKI SHOTEI HAD LAID siege to Shibata Katsuie's castle and had cut off the water supply. The garrison's morale was low, and it seemed only a matter of time before the castle fell.

At this point, an envoy was sent from Shotei's camp to find out how things stood inside the castle. Although by now water supplies were very low indeed, the garrison concealed this fact by using water lavishly, giving the impression that the castle still had plenty of water and could withstand the siege for a long time.

After the envoy left, Katsuie had the remaining water casks brought out, gave everyone a drink, and then had the casks smashed. "We are warriors!" he told his men. "Should we sit down and wait for death to come to us? No! If we are to die, let us die a warrior's death of dignity and glory!" The next morning, before dawn, Katsuie and his men burst out of the castle gates and hacked their way through the enemy lines. With courage born of despair, they defeated Shotei's forces and won a resounding victory.

*   *   *

Everyone holds life dear. No one wants to die. But if you are too preoccupied with your personal survival, you will not be able to perform to the peak of your abilities. Admittedly, it is not easy to argue that your own survival is not the top priority. Shibata Katsuie managed this feat by using shock tactics: he smashed the casks that literally contained the water of life.

When Katsuie burst out of the castle, resolutely facing the prospect of death, he and his men suffered casualties, but the final result was a decisive victory. This strategy may be called "reason beyond reason."

In normal circumstances, it is important to place a high value on life, material things, and money. If you try to hold on to these things when faced with a major crisis, however, you are likely to lose them. In an emergency, you must have the courage to cope by resigning yourself to losing your valuables, your money, or even your life. You could go even further, and deliberately sacrifice them if you thought you had a fighting chance. With this courageous outlook, you might end up losing only half of what you would lose taking any other approach. Then again, you might not lose anything, and perhaps even gain considerably.

This phenomenon is not amenable to logical analysis, but it is one of those truths that has been borne out time and time again throughout history. As such, it is something for a leader to bear in mind.

10

Don't Panic

A leader must keep
a cool head, especially during
an emergency

WHILE TOYOTOMI HIDEYOSHI AND Tokugawa Ieyasu were fighting at Komaki, Hideyoshi decided to lead 20,000 men in a surprise attack on Ieyasu's home ground of Mikawa. Ieyasu, however, got wind of this desperate stratagem and routed Hideyoshi's troops en route.

Hideyoshi's troops had been scouting the road ahead of them and did not even consider the possibility that they might be attacked from the rear. Taken by surprise, their ranks were thrown into disarray and their commanders cut off. The commander-in-chief—Hideyoshi's nephew—had his horse shot out from under him and barely escaped with his life in the crushing defeat.

Among the commanders of the vanquished army, one man distinguished himself: Hori Hidemasa. Hidemasa, suspecting that the enemy was planning an ambush, calmly mustered his troops and gave the following order: "Wait until the enemy is within twenty paces, then all fire together. I'll increase your stipend by a hundred *koku* for every horseman you hit!"

Those of Ieyasu's forces who met with this unified resistance were beaten back, leaving several hundred dead behind them. As the enemy fled, Hidemasa admonished his men not to chase them too far. Regrouping his troops, he brought them back safely to Hideyoshi's headquarters.

* * *

The way Hori Hidemasa handled this situation illustrates how important a leader's behavior is in an emergency. In the face of adversity, all men will feel fear and confusion. If a leader panics, then his panic will spread to the ranks, snowballing into uncontrollable chaos. But if the leader keeps calm and is clearly in control of the situation, this inspires confidence and courage in all under his command, enabling him to avoid confusion and maintain order when chaos threatens.

Of course, a leader is also a human being, so he will sometimes feel anxiety and confusion, but he cannot afford to let these private feelings show. Subordinates are extremely sensitive to their leader's attitude, and this quickly communicates itself to everyone inside the organization. If a leader shows weakness, the morale of the whole organization will suffer.

It is vital, therefore, that a leader cultivates the ability to keep a cool head in his everyday affairs, and also takes care to react calmly in the face of any difficulty.

11

Playing Fair

A leader should be wary of excessive competition

SOME 2,500 YEARS AGO, the Chinese sage Mo Zi re-marked, "The thing that does the most harm in the world is that nation attacks nation, tribe pillages tribe, and man murders his fellow man.

"This originates from our failure to love one another. We know how to love our own country, but not other countries. We know how to love our own tribe, but not other tribes. We know how to love ourselves, but not others. When we fail to love one another, the weak are overpowered by the strong, the poor are scorned by the rich, men of humble birth are despised by the nobility, and the foolish are cheated by the cunning. Almost all the mischief and enmity in the world arises from our failure to love one another. It is important to love one another and to do good to one another."

*   *   *

If Mo Zi's advice had been put into practice, we would no doubt be living in a wonderful world today. Things have not turned out that way because people have not really understood how important Mo Zi's insight was, and so have not taken it to heart.

I believe that Mo Zi's saying can also be read as a warning against what I call excessive competition. Appropriate competition—competition which abides by the rules of fairness—is a good thing, and leads to progress and improvement. Excessive competition, on the other hand, is competition with no regard for the rules, and in which one party seeks to overcome another by sheer brute force.

When two nations engage in excessive competition, this leads to war. Excessive competition between companies leads to high-handed use of capital and can result in the bankruptcy of smaller businesses. Excessive competition between individuals leads to quarrels and fights, and sometimes to murder. Excessive competition damages the other party and can throw a whole society, even the whole world, into chaos.

If we take the time to consider one another's interests, love our neighbor as we love ourselves, and love other countries as we love our own, this will lead to true peace, happiness, and prosperity.

Take this lesson to heart, eliminate excessive competition, and follow the rules of fair play.

12

You Can't Fight Human Nature

---

*A leader must
accept the world
for what it is*

THE FIRST ARTICLE OF Prince Shotoku's Seventeen-Article Constitution, said to have been promulgated in 604, is entitled, "Be gentle in your dealings with others. Make it a rule to avoid confrontation, because everyone has his own allegiances."

*   *   *

Human beings are social animals who naturally form groups. These groups vary in size, ranging from small cliques to huge conglomerates, and most people belong to more than one group.

Within an organization, the groups or factions that form can be harmful to it. This is particularly true of government, where a good deal of effort has been expended in trying to break up factions, with very little result. It is a fruitless exercise trying to prevent groups from forming, so the best way to deal with factions is to acknowledge their existence and utilize them somehow.

This is what Prince Shotoku meant by, "Be gentle in your dealings with others." He is advising us not to become too preoccupied with factions but to concentrate on the well-being of the organization as a whole.

This was his genius. Basic human nature is not something we can change. We may try and try, but our efforts will be in vain and, much worse, they will probably cause unhappiness. Only by acknowledging this point and accepting it can we get on with life.

Putting Prince Shotoku's advice into practice, however, is easier said than done. We are influenced by our likes and dislikes and by our natural desire to arrange things for our own convenience. These factors cloud our judgment and cause us to make mistakes.

As a leader you must make every effort to avoid being influenced by your personal feelings, and instead must confront things as they really are. Unless you are in touch with reality, you cannot begin to lead effectively.

13

Listening to Criticism

A good leader would rather hear bad news than good

ONE DAY SOMEONE POSTED a large placard in front of Hori Hidemasa's castle, listing up the shortcomings of the government for all to see. The castle officials held a meeting to discuss the affront, eventually showing the placard to Hidemasa with the words, "We must arrest and execute the person who wrote this without delay."

Hori Hidemasa carefully studied what was written on the placard. Then, to the amazement of all present, he put on his most formal attire, ceremoniously rinsed his mouth and hands, and raised the placard above his head in reverence. "No one has ever given me advice like this," he said. "I regard this placard as a gift from the gods and will keep it among my family treasures." He placed the placard inside a finely-wrought bag and locked it safely in a chest. Then he got down to business with his officials, discussed each grievance listed, and set about reforming the government accordingly.

* * *

A leader should turn to his associates for opinions and information about the way things are going as a matter of course. He should always listen to the bad news more closely than the good. If the news is good and reports say that all is going well, then all he needs to do is listen. But when he hears about problems and proposed solutions, he must be prepared to take action. If, as leader, you never get to hear about these things, or don't listen closely enough, then much needed action may never be taken.

In practice, subordinates tend to protect leaders from bad news. If good news makes the leader happy and bad news makes him mad, why deliver the bad, they reason.

Tokugawa Ieyasu, the first Tokugawa shogun, used to say that criticism was worth more than the best lance. The samurai prizes his best lance amongst all his weaponry, yet Ieyasu placed even greater value on the gift of advice to a lord—perhaps one of the hardest things to give.

A leader must actively seek as much advice and bad news as possible, and create an atmosphere in which it is easy for people to report bad tidings. Hori Hidemasa recognized the importance of this and behaved accordingly.

14

Give Thanks

A leader must have a deep sense of gratitude for all things

SHINRAN, FOUNDER OF THE Jodo-Shin sect of Pure Land Buddhism, was a truly great man, yet he called himself Stupid Shinran because he saw himself as an incorrigible sinner who could not conquer his evil desires. Shinran believed with conviction that even sinners like himself could be saved by the Original Vow of Amida Buddha, and he taught people the importance of chanting the Buddha's name in heartfelt thanks for their salvation.

* * *

A sense of gratitude in a person is very important. No man can live entirely off his wits alone. We did not create the abundant natural resources we need to survive. Every individual's work depends on the cooperation of other people. In other words, we owe our daily lives to the blessings of nature and the goodwill of our fellow man.

It is important to be aware of this, to feel deep gratitude, and to repay the kindness of others. Do so, and you release a source of limitless energy.

An expression of gratitude increases the value of things. If you perceive somebody's gift as a trifle, you attach very little value to it. But if you appreciate it, its value will seem proportionately greater and you will be able to make better use of it. Remember that a thankful heart can turn lead into gold.

If you have little capacity to appreciate, then you will become resentful and discontented for no good reason. This will give you a jaundiced outlook and make you liable to hurt others. On the other hand, a strong sense of appreciation will help you find something good in everything, making you light-hearted and at peace with others. In this state of mind, you will find it easy to follow the old adage, live and let live.

Gratitude is an excellent quality to cultivate, and it is particularly important in a leader. When all leaders attain this state of mind, we shall see the birth of a world which is truly prosperous in a material and spiritual sense.

15

Gut Feelings

**A leader must
cultivate his powers
of intuition**

WHILE INSPECTING THE FRONT lines during the Russo-Japanese war, General Kuroki Tametomo often remarked, "There will be an attack tonight!" Sure enough, every time he made that prediction the enemy would attack that very evening.

* * *

The general was certain of the attack not because he had special information but because he had a gut feeling that an attack was in store. He had, so to speak, a "sixth sense."

At first, the idea of a sixth sense seems unscientific and irrational. But this only makes it all the more important for a leader to cultivate.

Consider this example. It is said that Newton discovered the force of gravity when he observed an apple fall. Newton was definitely not the first man to have seen an apple drop. But nobody before Newton had noticed anything unusual in this phenomenon. It was Newton who thought, "That's odd. There's something interesting going on here!"

This is what is known as intuition. Scientific research often starts off with intuition, as with Newton and the apple or Archimedes and his bath. Without intuition, it would no doubt be difficult for scientists to make any great breakthroughs.

As a leader, you need a leader's intuition, the ability to judge a situation based on your gut feelings. If you are a merchant, you have to be able to tell at a glance whether a given product will sell and what it is worth. It is no good finding out by trial and error.

So, how do you go about acquiring this intuition? You do this through experience and gradual self-teaching.

The famous swordsmen of old are said to have second-guessed their opponent's movements using their intuition, dodging the swordpoint by a hair's breadth. They achieved this level of skill by constant and often bloody practice.

Practice strict self-discipline and draw on your experience to cultivate the sixth sense that will enable you to divine the truth. By combining this intuition with rational thinking, you will be able to achieve great results.

16

Turn Higher Powers to Your Own Advantage

A leader must sometimes appeal to a greater authority

BEFORE ODA NOBUNAGA FOUGHT Imagawa Yoshimoto at the battle of Okehazama, he assembled his troops in front of Atsuta shrine. As he was offering up prayers for victory, everyone present heard the sound of clashing weapons from behind the main shrine building. Turning to his troops, Nobunaga said, "Did you hear that? That was a sign that the gods have heard our prayers and have granted us their protection!" This gave a tremendous boost to his troops, and they went on to win a famous victory.

*   *   *

Oda Nobunaga probably believed in the Shinto and Buddhist deities, but it is unlikely that he believed the noise from behind the shrine was really a sign from the gods. A decisive commander, it is more likely that he seized the opportunity to encourage his troops and raise their fighting spirit.

Imagawa Yoshimoto's ranks at the battle of Oke-hazama were greatly swelled by his allies, and defeat for Nobunaga seemed all but assured. Perhaps his miraculous victory should be attributed to the fact that he invoked the power of the gods to fill his soldiers with courage.

As a leader, you should be able to invoke the power of a higher authority in this way. In many cases, it is more persuasive than relying on your own word.

Religion offers many such examples. When preaching, priests and other religious leaders never present their arguments as their own personal ideas. Instead, they say "Buddha said...," or "Christ taught that..." This method of teaching is much more persuasive.

If such a power is available in your society, you should use this authority as a starting point. Do not mislead anyone, but use the tenets of this belief system to back up your own arguments. This will prove a very effective reinforcement.

You can use Shinto and Buddhism, the teachings of some great leader, traditional myths, or the philosophy of your organization, but be prepared to invoke the power of a higher authority. You should not misuse this power, but use it to give weight to your message. If there is no such authority already in existence, you must try and create one.

17

Demand the Best

A leader must set strict standards

UMEWAKA MINORU WAS A famous Noh performer. In his youth he studied daily under a teacher called Yamashina Takigoro. On one occasion, Takigoro made the young Minoru repeat a certain section of a Noh chant over and over, refusing to be satisfied with his pupil's performance. When the boy asked what he was doing wrong, the teacher would not tell him, but simply made him chant it over and over "until he got it right."

Minoru repeated the chant until tears were running down his cheeks, but still Takigoro would not give his approval. At some stage, the youth suddenly noticed that his teacher had left the room. Taking this for a sign that the day's lesson was over, he went home. Takigoro returned shortly afterward, and asked his servants where the boy was. On hearing that he had gone home, the master flew into a rage and vowed never to give the boy another lesson. A somewhat bemused Minoru apologized abjectly to his teacher and eventually obtained forgiveness and further training.

* * *

This is what it means to "suffer for one's art." All famous luminaries in every discipline have reached excellence only by undergoing training as rigorous as that of Umewaka Minoru. If you are in the position of being a mentor, you must be as strict as Yamashina Takigoro.

It is absolutely indispensable for leaders to be strict. A leader deals in public affairs, not personal ones, and must work for the good of society, not for his own sake.

Never lose sight of this fact. Always be strict with yourself and those under your command. From a personal viewpoint, this may seem harsh, and there may be times when you cannot find it in your heart to be this way. But to get things done, a leader must suppress his personal feelings. He must be strict but equitable, push all subordinates to the limit, and sternly reprimand anyone who slacks off.

This is the implicit demand that the world makes of a leader. Unless he is capable of exercising strictness in his official position, he won't be able to train his subordinates or realize his goals.

18

Keep Your Resolve

A leader must constantly renew his determination to succeed

DURING CHINA'S SPRING AND Autumn period, King He Lu of Wu was defeated by King Gou Xian of Yue, and died of the wounds he received in battle. With his dying breath, He Lu charged his son, Fu Cha, to conquer Gou Xian and settle the score. From then on, Fu Cha slept on a pile of firewood every night to strengthen his resolve to crush his father's enemy. He built up an army and took every opportunity to harass his adversary, eventually conquering Yue and Gou Xian within three years.

But the story doesn't end there. For although badly beaten, Gou Xian managed to survive the encounter and now resolved to obtain vengeance for himself. He nursed his grudge, savored his bitterness, and twelve long years later managed to defeat Fu Cha, who had become complacent in his victory.

*   *   *

It is important for a leader to have a definite goal in mind and achieve it by the only means possible, resolute determination to pursue that goal. This does not mean that once you have set yourself a goal, you can achieve it merely by making up your mind to do so— you have to maintain your determination and keep your guard up, which is where Fu Cha failed. To this end, you must constantly spur yourself on, keeping your resolve fresh.

In the beginning, when his commitment was fresh, Fu Cha lay on a hard floor atop an uncomfortable bed of knobbly firewood. Throughout his sleepless nights, he nursed his grievance and dreamed of avenging his father's death. But when he had achieved that objective, he dropped his guard and was subsequently defeated by Gou Xian. The story is a classic example of human frailty.

Anyone can achieve great things by setting a goal and working toward it with unrelenting determination. But it is common for people to let their determination dissipate, and fail to see all things through to the end.

Although a leader does not necessarily have to sleep on a bed of firewood or nurse a bitter desire for revenge, one of the most important mental exercises he must develop is to keep his resolve fresh.

19

Be Bold

A leader needs the drive to act decisively

AFTER HIS FIRST MAJOR strategic victory at the battle of Okehazama in 1560, Oda Nobunaga still had only two domains under his control. All around him, stronger opponents held their ground and maintained a fierce front. But even in these circumstances, Nobunaga had the strength of character to take his sword in hand and set about the task of subduing these warlords, thereby bringing peace to the country. Here was a man who embodied the very concept of "drive."

Oda Nobunaga's drive is illustrated by the order he gave to burn Enryakuji temple to the ground. Enryakuji was the headquarters of the Tendai sect of Buddhism, and its warrior monks stood in the way of Nobunaga's ambition. Akechi Mitsuhide and Nobunaga's other retainers pleaded with him not to burn what had been sacred since the time of Emperor Kanmu, but Nobunaga dismissed their advice. "Since I stand for the reunification of the nation," he said, "I am following the decrees of the Emperor Kanmu in my heart, and I shall obtain the forgiveness of Saicho [the long-dead founder of the sect] before I do this."

"If I am to be punished and cast into the fires of hell, I am confident that I could win my case in the courts of hell before the Devil himself." Seeing his resolution in the face of such fearsome possibilities, his retainers acquiesced, and the temple was razed.

* * *

History's view of the burning of Enryakuji temple is mixed. It is said that Oda Nobunaga's ruthlessness eventually caused Mitsuhide to rise up in rebellion. Perhaps Oda Nobunaga was given to excess, but it was thanks to his drive that long years of wartime chaos and widespread misery came to an end, and an era of peace dawned upon Japan which lasted three hundred years.

"Act resolutely, and both heaven and hell will respect you," the saying goes. As a leader, when you make up your mind to do something, you must have the determination to carry it out.

These days, it is rarely appropriate to use force of arms to get one's way. It is also true that you can take a good idea too far. But there is an object lesson for every leader in the iron determination with which Oda Nobunaga held his ground and proceeded as he thought best for the common good.

20

Who's to Blame?

---

*A leader must look
within himself for the cause
of any failure*

IN THE MEIREKI FIRE of 1657, Edo Castle and the
surrounding area suffered terrible damage. Some government officials handled the situation very well, but
many panicked, not knowing what to do. Shortly afterward, the country's leaders met to take disciplining
action and make sure this wouldn't happen again.

The senior minister, Hoshina Masayuki, addressed
his colleagues. "It's of great importance to ensure this
doesn't happen again, but to mete out punishment
without having given clear instructions about what to
do in such a situation would be irresponsible," he said.
"We have just experienced the biggest fire for seventy
years. We had no contingency plans for such a confla-
gration and were reduced to a state of chaos. If we
really care about the future, we should first learn some-

thing from this experience. We should go away and individually consider what to do in the event of a major fire." With that, the meeting dissolved.

*   *   *

When a mistake is made or a problem arises, the natural tendency is to look for an external cause. We tend to blame failure on someone else, on society, or on bad luck. In practice, however, the cause of failure most often lies within ourselves.

You minimize the chances of a careless mistake through proper planning and attention to the plan's execution. The leader is then fully responsible for what happens. If a follower makes a mistake, it is also the leader's mistake. The leader must ask himself, "Did I choose the right person for the task?" and, "Was he given enough guidance and training?"

This was the thrust of Hoshina Masayuki's speech. He didn't blame the junior officials for their inability to deal with the blaze, he felt the responsibility to be his own and that of the other ministers, because they had failed to formulate an appropriate fire drill. Consequently, he was able to forgive the mistakes of his junior officials.

Provided that you plan thoroughly, take all contingencies into account, and proceed with due caution, it is possible to minimize mistakes. As a leader, you must be fully aware of this fact. If a follower makes a mistake, apportion blame, but also remember to accept responsibility yourself.

21

Be Humble

The higher a leader's position, the more humble he should be

MAEDA TOSHIIE ONCE RECEIVED a present of two carp from Fukushima Masanori. Toshiie, a prominent lord, had his retainer write a letter of thanks, which the retainer wrote in a very brief, pro forma style because Toshiie was of higher status. When he saw the letter, Toshiie said, "Public documents may be written to a set format, but a letter like this should be written in a courteous, respectful tone, thanking the giver for his kindness. If the giver is a person of lower rank, then the more polite the letter, the more pleasure it will bring to the recipient. A condescending letter to a person of lower status will only emphasize the gulf between your own status and his, and make him look foolish." With that, he had the retainer rewrite the letter.

*   *   *

Maeda Toshiie was a heroic general, ranking with Oda Nobunaga and Toyotomi Hideyoshi, but he was also a sincere man and very popular with the people. It is even said that if such a man had been alive during Tokugawa Ieyasu's time, Ieyasu would not have become shogun. The source of Toshiie's great popularity lay in his rise to a high position without becoming haughty, arrogant, or overproud. He remained unassuming and humble in his dealings with others.

The higher a man rises, the greater the tendency of those around him to express respect for the position of office, rather than for the person in that position. As a person becomes accustomed to high status, the natural tendency is to become haughty and arrogant. When this happens, people may continue to pay lip service, but they will gradually lose any respect for the person and cease to admire him. When this happens to a leader, he becomes unable to motivate people or exert strong leadership.

However high the position, a leader must not lose a sense of humility. Indeed, the higher he rises, the more vital it is that a leader remain humble. A humble person generates genuine respect in those he encounters. People are grateful for a lack of pomposity and appreciate courtesy from above. A humble leader also listens to what people say, and so is able to gather information from many sources. As the old saying goes, "The heaviest ears of rice bow the lowest."

22

Allocating Responsibility

A leader must assign tasks according to ability

ODA NOBUNAGA WAS MAKING a tour of his fief and a young man called Kinoshita Tokichiro happened to be part of the entourage. The group came to Nobunaga's castle and studied repairs being made to walls that had collapsed some twenty days before. Tokichiro was heard to remark, "These days, when the country is at war and the enemy could attack at any moment, we cannot allow repairs to drag on like this." Nobunaga was so struck by this that he made the young man shogunate administrator on the spot.

Appalled at the disorganized manner in which construction was proceeding, Tokichiro drew up a completely new work schedule. He divided the repair work into different sections, made separate work groups responsible for repairs in their section, and went around the groups encouraging them in their tasks. In this fashion the work was completed in barely two days. Nobunaga was greatly impressed, commended the young man highly, and increased his stipend.

*   *   *

Kinoshita Tokichiro's approach was very similar to the methods commonly used in modern business management. Before he reorganized them, large numbers of artisans had been tackling the task in a generally haphazard fashion. The result was an inefficient work schedule and no clear picture of how the work was actually progressing. By dividing the task up into manageable-sized jobs and establishing clear lines of responsibility, Tokichiro ensured that the task could be carried out without further delay and that he could keep track of overall progress. The young man, by the way, was later known as Toyotomi Hideyoshi, who was to complete Nobunaga's task of reunifying Japan.

It is very important to proceed in this way: divide the job into manageable portions, allocate responsibility for each portion, and encourage workers to work methodically. One man by himself can only accomplish so much. If a person attempts something beyond his capacities, he will surely fail. Assign tasks to people in accordance with their capabilities. If the task is too much for one person to tackle alone, divide it up among several people.

This is what a leader must bear in mind. He must allocate responsibility so that tasks are assigned to persons (or groups) in accordance with their capabilities.

23

Knowing What Comes Next

A leader has to look beyond his nose

AFTER MINAMOTO YORITOMO SUFFERED a resounding defeat in the battle of Ishibashiyama at Izu, he retreated with his remaining soldiers to Awa province. Hoping to rally his forces, he urged the local samurai to join him. Some powerful domains promptly rallied to his cause, but Yoritomo was disappointed to find that the most powerful domain, led by Chiba Hirotsune, was not among them. With no time to argue, the small band of troops set out, much depleted by the absence of the missing clan. A little later, however, they were joined by Hirotsune and his men, which boosted their numbers by some 20,000.

As Yoritomo's troop was only a few thousand strong, 20,000 men made an enormous difference. Instead of expressing great joy at his ally's appearance, however,

Yoritomo turned on Hirotsune, chiding him for his tardiness and demanding an explanation for the delay. Hirotsune was taken aback, as were the other clans, who made excuses on his behalf. But Yoritomo was adamant. The vacillating Hirotsune was obliged to swear devotion to Yoritomo and pledge his sincere loyalty. With this, the enlarged army set forth to achieve victory at a single stroke.

* * *

An ally who can field 20,000 men is a powerful ally indeed. Under normal circumstances, one would expect Minamoto Yoritomo to have been effusively grateful to Chiba Hirotsune for joining him. But what would have been the eventual outcome had he done this? For one thing, the other distinguished samurai who had rushed to his aid with their troops would have felt rather insulted. For another, Hirotsune, aware of his own strength, might have defied Yoritomo's orders and acted on his own initiative. If this had happened, the whole army—now tens of thousands strong—would have lost discipline and degenerated into an unruly rabble.

People generally judge things in terms of quantity and power—large or small quantity and strong or weak power. This approach is certainly not wrong. Ignoring comparative measurements in normal circumstances is to court disaster. This is the case when dealing with everyday matters, but when major decisions must be made, a leader must look beyond his nose, beyond the immediate gains and losses, to avoid making mistakes. A discerning mind is the leader's key.

24

One Law for All

A leader must strive for impartiality in all aspects of public life

DURING CHINA'S SPRING AND Autumn period, the kingdom of Qin gradually gained enough power to unite the whole country. Qin's ascendancy was largely due to a minister called Shang Yang, who drew up a strict code of law for governing the country.

It happened one day that the crown prince of Qin was found to be in breach of Shang Yang's laws. After giving the matter some consideration, Shang Yang announced that no breach of the law, even by a crown prince, could be tolerated, then severely punished the crown prince's retainers and tutors. Since such a case had never happened before, the people were greatly impressed and, from that time onward, they upheld the law. This left Qin free from crime and disorder, its subjects prospered and the country was at peace.

*   *   *

Shang Yang's fairness in administering justice was the key to his success. If the common people are punished for their transgressions, while the misdemeanors of those in high places go unpunished, no one feels any genuine desire to uphold the law. People may pay lip service to the law, but they will resent its unfair application, and eventually lose respect for it.

Modern Japan is a democracy and the law is supposed to be applied even-handedly. But I wonder if this is really the case. The system certainly deals with individual breaches of the law, but when large numbers of people combine into a faceless group and commit crimes or apply unfair pressure to advance their cause, responsibility is difficult to pinpoint and so such infringements tend to be overlooked. Hence the law is applied strictly to the weak, while the strong somehow get off more easily. But when the law is applied unfairly it is as if there were no law. People are bound to become disaffected and the social order will break down.

This problem is not confined to the legal system: it also exists in the corporate world. When company regulations are upheld from the company president down to the newest recruit and when all persons who infringe these regulations are punished equally, the integrity of the system is upheld and morale rises dramatically.

25

The Need for Integrity

As a leader, you must monitor your own behavior and keep your conscience clear

---

IN CHINA'S LATER HAN era, there lived a politician called Yang Zhen, a man known for his upright character. After Yang Zhen was made a provincial governor, one of his earlier patrons, Wang Mi, paid him an unexpected visit. As they talked over old times, Wang Mi brought out a large gold cup and presented it to Yang Zhen. Yang Zhen refused to accept it, but Wang Mi persisted, saying, "There's no one here tonight but you and me, so no one will know."

"You say that no one will know," Yang Zhen replied, "but that is not true. Heaven will know, and you and I will know too."

Wang Mi was ashamed, and backed down. Subsequently Yang Zhen's integrity won increasing recognition, and he rose to a high post in the central government.

* * *

Human nature is weak, and we tend to yield to temptation when we think nobody can see us. In fact, if there was no police force, many people would not hesitate to steal. This is not to say that when we do something bad, we feel no compunction at all, just that man is weak and prone to yield to temptation.

But even if nobody witnesses our sins, and not a soul knows of them, we cannot hide the truth from the eyes of our conscience. In the end, what is important is not that other people know, but that we ourselves know. When Yang Zhen told Wang Mi that "Heaven will know," he meant that the gods would know what he had done: in other words, his own conscience.

A man who sins neither in thought nor deed, and is fair and just, gains enormous courage and strength. As a leader, you need courage born of integrity in order to be capable of powerful leadership. To achieve this courage, you must search your heart, and make sure that your conscience is clear and your behavior is beyond reproach.

26

Be Ambitious

A leader must set his sights high

IN 1876, DR. WILLIAM CLARK, president of Massachusetts Agricultural College, was invited to take up the post of vice-principal at the newly established Sapporo Agricultural College, now part of Hokkaido University. He served in the position for eight months, and several of his proteges, such as Sato Shosuke, Uchimura Kanzo, and Nitobe Inazo, went on to become great educators.

According to one of his students, as Dr. Clark was about to ride off he turned in his saddle and shouted in farewell, "Boys, be ambitious!"

* * *

When we start out in life, it is most important to have

ambition. Confucius said, "At the age of fifteen I set my heart on learning"; Nichiren's ambition at the age of twelve was to become "the wisest man in Japan." You can set yourself a life goal to strive for, or you can set a series of smaller goals throughout your life. Ambition can take various forms, but if you have no ambition, merely living from day to day, life becomes less enjoyable and less meaningful.

By setting yourself a goal, however, you develop strength in the process of trying to achieve it. If this is true for a private individual, then it is naturally even more important for a leader. When a leader has an ambition and explains it to his people, everyone develops a strong sense of purpose as they work toward this goal. If a leader has no ambition, his people cannot focus on the path they should follow.

When deciding on your goal, be ambitious. This does not mean that your ambition should be a dream totally divorced from reality; rather, you should be reaching for something just beyond your grasp. Only by having ambitious goals and aiming high can you hope to achieve anything out of the ordinary. If you start out with only limited ambition, you may fail to achieve even what is already within reach.

In this sense, Dr. Clark's words are still extremely relevant if we rephrase them slightly: "Leaders, be ambitious!"

27

Never Switch Off

*A leader's mind should
always be at work, even when
his body is at rest*

ARCHIMEDES, THE GREAT GREEK mathematician, was once ordered to examine a gold crown and find out whether the gold had been adulterated. There was a rumor that the craftsman who had fashioned the crown from a solid gold bar had been dishonest.

Not permitted to break up the crown and analyze it, Archimedes was at a loss what to do. One day, however, when he was at the public bathhouse, he was suddenly struck by the way the water ran over the sides of his bathtub. He then realized that he could solve the problem of the crown by submerging it and measuring the amount of water displaced; he could then compare this with the amount displaced by an equal weight of pure gold. Overjoyed, he rushed stark naked from the bathhouse, shouting "Eureka! Eureka!" He immediately carried out the experiment and was able to prove that the gold in the crown had, in fact, been adulterated.

* * *

How ardently Archimedes pursued the truth, and racked his brains for a solution! It seems that he couldn't take his mind off the problem for even a minute. Even when he took a relaxing bath to refresh himself, his mind didn't stop working. When he saw the overflowing water, he had a flash of inspiration, and grasped the solution to his problem.

It is just as important for a leader to keep his mind working. This is not to say that a leader is obliged to work day and night without any relief. That would be extremely bad for the health. You should take regular breaks, relax, and enjoy your leisure. Although it is fine to rest your body, however, it will not do to relax your mind. Your mind must never stop working.

Suppose you go to a spa to relax. If you are a politician, you must keep thinking about political matters; if you are a manager, you must constantly think about management. If you do this, then, like Archimedes, you will be able to gain insights from phenomena as trivial as the way water flows over the sides of the bathtub.

The kind of man who lets his mind relax completely during his leisure, although he may appear to be highly disciplined, is not qualified to be a leader.

28

Overconfidence

**A leader must be
fully aware of the perils
of public office**

A YOUNG MAN WHO was training as a military tactician once requested an interview with master swordsman Miyamoto Musashi. Musashi met him, listened to what he had to say, looked him up and down, and complimented him with these words: "You seem a promising young man. I am sure you could serve as an advisor to any lord."

The young man suddenly drew his sword. "I shall travel around the domains, and use this when I am challenged to a fight," he said.

"You would not say such things if you were such a skillful fighter," Musashi retorted. He then summoned a page and had him kneel down. Next, he placed a grain of rice on the page's forelock, and took out his sword. "Watch this!" he said, and swinging his weapon he delicately cut the grain of rice clean in two without harming a hair of the page's head.

Turning to his visitor, he asked, "Can you do that?" The young man admitted that he could not, so Musashi scolded him. "Even if you were as skillful as that," he said, "you would still be no match for your enemy. Never enter into a fight rashly. A man who knows when to run away from a fight is a man who understands the essence of tactics."

* * *

Miyamoto Musashi never lost once in over sixty duels. How interesting, then, that he should make the above remark. He obviously had a healthy respect for danger.

This is something we all need. To live a better life, we have to discipline ourselves constantly and behave correctly. In order to do this, we must have respect for and stand in awe of certain people and certain things. A child is in awe of its parents, a pupil is in awe of the teacher, and a company employee is in awe of the president: human beings are motivated by a sense of caution to regulate their behavior. A man without caution is a man who often goes too far, making mistakes and hurting other people.

Leaders tend to lose their sense of circumspection because no one around them will criticize them directly. Let us examine this more closely. If you are a company president, say, or prime minister, then no one will criticize you to your face; but if you make a mistake, then public opinion will rebound on you.

Even a prime minister must have a healthy respect for his people, and must carry out his political activities without making mistakes. A sense of circumspection is very important in a leader.

57

29

Never Give Up

**A leader doesn't
throw in the towel when
there's still a chance**

DEFEATED AND CAPTURED at the battle of Sekigahara, Ishida Mitsunari was taken to Tokugawa Ieyasu's residence. Honda Masazumi, Ieyasu's retainer, heaped scorn on the captive for allowing himself to be taken prisoner rather than committing suicide. "Surely this is not the way a warrior should behave," he said. But Mitsunari replied, "Killing oneself to avoid capture is the common soldier's way out. A real general will not carelessly throw away his life: he will hang on to the bitter end, looking for an alternative."

Just before he was beheaded, someone offered him a persimmon, which he refused on the grounds that the fruit disagreed with him. Everyone laughed, but he explained, "I believe it is right to value my life highly up until the very moment of death. I do not intend to abandon the principles I have lived by."

*　*　*

Opinions have always varied on whether or not Mitsunari was wise to wage war on Ieyasu, and about the way he handled the battle. But we can all learn from his determination to remain true to his principles. As he reminded Honda Masazumi, the great warrior Minamoto Yoritomo had once hidden in the hollow trunk of a rotten tree when his life was in danger. Escaping by a hair's breadth, he survived, regrouped his army, and ended up becoming shogun.

If you set yourself a goal and begin working toward it, come what may, you must not give up just because you suffer a setback. If you are faint-hearted enough to let one or two failures put you off, you will never really accomplish anything. The world is in a constant state of change and flux. Even if you fail once, do not lose heart: as you keep on trying, patiently and steadily, the situation may change to your advantage, and new doors may open to you. Many so-called failures are the result of giving up too early.

Of course, I am not advocating stubborn persistence for its own sake. It is also very important to have the flexibility to adapt to changing circumstances. But as a leader, once you have fixed on a just cause, and set yourself an ambition, as long as there is still a chance, even if the odds are only one in a hundred, you should never give up.

30

Fostering Independence

**A leader must
encourage his followers
to think for themselves**

ANDO NAOTSUGU WAS SPECIALLY chosen by Tokugawa Ieyasu to act as guardian for his son. Naotsugu trained
the boy strictly, and had the satisfaction of seeing his
young charge grow into a wise and noble ruler.

A senior councilor, Doi Toshikatsu, visited Naotsugu
to learn about affairs of state. While Toshikatsu looked
on, various junior officials came to ask Naotsugu's
approval on a number of matters. All were answered
promptly with a simple "yes" or "no." Proposals that
had been modified and re-submitted would be turned
down time and time again with a curt "no" until Naotsugu was satisfied. Puzzled by this, Toshikatsu asked,
"Why just answer 'yes' or 'no'? Why not give your
subordinates more detailed instructions? Surely that
would speed things up."

"Of course," Naotsugu replied. "But if I gave them detailed instructions, they would rely on me, instead of thinking for themselves. That is not the way to train good officials." Toshikatsu learned much from this remark.

* * *

As a leader, you will often have to delegate work to people who are not fully trained. Their proposals and suggestions will contain shortcomings. Your natural impulse will be to deal with these shortcomings by telling your subordinates exactly how to put them right. On occasion, this is necessary, and you must give precise instructions.

Spoon-fed subordinates become complacent, however. They do as they are told, but they won't act unless you give them instructions. They will neither develop nor become capable of doing really useful work. The important thing is that they should have the independence to think, to make decisions, and to act on their own initiative. Not until your subordinates carry out their work with this independence can they truly make progress and achieve worthwhile results.

In today's fast-moving business world, there is no time to spell out every little detail. Be like Ando Naotsugu and encourage your subordinates to think things out for themselves. Don't let them turn into automata, simply acting on your orders.

31

See Things for What They Are

---

*A leader must never
let personal considerations
cloud his judgment*

WHEN THE FIRST MEIJI government was formed in the late 1860s, those filling the top positions were drawn from the most distinguished domains, chief among them Satsuma and Choshu. Disputes arose from time to time, preventing the work of government from proceeding smoothly.

Observing this state of affairs, Saigo Takamori of the Satsuma domain concluded, "In government, too many cooks spoil the broth. Let us appoint Kido Takayoshi [of Choshu] to act as chief councilor, and the rest of us will be subordinate to him." The others agreed, except for Kido himself, who insisted that, while he was willing to act as chief councilor alongside Saigo, under no circumstances would he undertake the task alone. All present urged Saigo to accept the post, and eventually the two men became joint chief councilors, combining their strength to resolve complex issues.

Saigo had previous experience of the antagonism between the Satsuma and Choshu domains. On that occasion, he proposed that both follow the leadership of Omura Masujiro of Choshu. This eventually happened, and had the effect of uniting the two sides.

* * *

Among the patriots of the Meiji Restoration were many men who disregarded their own interests entirely and worked tirelessly for the good of the nation. Even in this company, however, Saigo Takamori's complete lack of self-interest was outstanding. All who came in contact with him saw him as a great man and a charismatic figure, and no one would have found it strange if he had become supreme leader. Instead, he made himself subordinate to another leader and obliged everyone else to obey that leader too. In this way, he ensured that things ran smoothly.

Self-regard and self-love are a part of everyone's psychic make-up, and are perfectly natural feelings. If you allow yourself to be swayed by these feelings, however, your judgment will become clouded, and you won't benefit from powerful inspiration. Only when you abandon selfish motives, seek the truth, and do what has to be done, will you feel the power of inspiration and courage welling up within you.

Disinterested vision is a desirable quality in all human beings, but it is especially important in a leader. You may not be able to reach the heights scaled by Saigo Takamori, but in your capacity as a leader, you should aim for a balance of 40 percent self-interest to 60 percent disinterested altruism.

32

Believe in Something

**A leader needs
a philosophy to back up
his leadership**

How do you lead a country the size of China, with a population of more than 1 billion? Chairman Mao Zedong had his famous, 'Little Red Book,' which contained sayings that acted as a national code of conduct, playing a fundamental role in the running of the country and the regulation of the nation's activities. In short, China had an explicit set of basic principles behind its leadership. The way ahead and the steps to be taken were clearly formulated.

This happened because China's leader at that time, Chairman Mao Zedong, had clear ideas on these subjects. Each time he held a meeting, Chairman Mao would always formulate a clear agenda. For example, the day after the Sino-Japanese war began in 1937, he is said to have formulated an eight-point plan for the conduct of war as well as the "Three Principles and Eight Items" for the People's Liberation Army. The army's activities were conducted according to this policy.

China had an ideology of leadership in the form of Mao Zedong's philosophy, which was the reference point for case-by-case formulation of specific policies. This is the ideology which united that huge country, mobilized its 1 billion people, and enabled it to maintain steady progress. This ideology was the keystone of Mao Zedong's greatness as a leader.

* * *

If you are a leader, you must have an ideology of leadership. If you lack an ideology, and attempt to decide everything on a case-by-case basis, you will never be capable of strong leadership. If you are the leader of a nation, you must have a political philosophy, and if you are a manager, you must have a management philosophy. Of course, every country has a constitution, and every company has a certificate of incorporation, in which the basic nature of the nation or the company are stated. But it is the leader's ideology of leadership which brings to life the constitution or the certificate of incorporation, and enables the leader to manage the real nation or the real company. The point I would like to make is this: an ideology of leadership, used as a basis on which to formulate concrete policies for day-to-day situations, is a tower of strength and a foundation for real growth and development.

33

Know Your Limitations

A leader must have a ready grasp of his own strengths and weaknesses

TOYOTOMI HIDEYOSHI SET OUT to conquer Kyushu and Shikoku, and then went on to subdue western Japan. This achieved, he sent a message to the Hojo family, the most powerful rulers in the Kanto region, requiring them to submit. But not realizing that Hideyoshi dominated the country, and overestimating their own strength, the Hojo ignored Hideyoshi's message and disregarded his orders, which gave Hideyoshi the pretext to wage war.

The outcome of the battle was obvious from the start. Although the Hojo forces had many past victories to their credit, they were unable to prevail against Hideyoshi, who could muster half the country's troops. Faced by such overwhelming odds, the house of Hojo was destroyed.

*　*　*

In the words of Confucius, "A man who knows his enemy and knows himself will never lose a battle." Clearly, the Hojo knew neither. Centuries later, Japan underestimated U.S. strength, and overestimated its own, when it engaged the United States in the Pacific War.

Of course, as well as accurately estimating your own and your enemy's strength, you must determine when is the time for battle and when is the time for reconciliation. Admittedly, this is easier said than done. People tend to hope for the best, underestimate their adversaries, and be overconfident about their own abilities. It is difficult enough to gauge your opponent's strength, but even more difficult to know your own. Our own abilities should be the easiest things for us to gauge, but in fact we tend to see ourselves in a very subjective way.

As a leader, you must take full account of this. To obtain an accurate assessment of your own strength and the strength of your own company, organization, or nation, you must study them objectively. Know yourself well, and you will be able to weigh up your adversary. Once you have this skill, you will rarely fail in your undertakings, whatever they may be.

34

A Sense of Mission

A leader derives strength from a sense of purpose

NICHIREN WAS A GREAT religious leader who unflaggingly spread the Buddha's teachings. He never deviated from his chosen path, even in the face of severe hardship and persecution. As well as spreading the word among the common people, he also preached to the government of the Kamakura shogunate. In the course of this work, his hermitage was burned down, he was arrested by the shogunate, tortured to within an inch of his life, then banished to Sado Island in the Japan Sea. But throughout indescribable hardships, he continued steadfast in his mission, never wavering in his firm belief in the Buddha's teachings.

* * *

Where did Nichiren derive such strength? The answer, I believe, is from his sense of mission. He lived in tumultuous times—natural disasters and upheavals followed one upon the next, and society was in a continuous state of chaos. Nichiren believed that this was because men had lost sight of the true teachings of Buddha. He saw the spreading of the word as a mission that had been entrusted to him, and this gave him the strength to live up to his task.

"I shall be Japan's pillar, I shall be Japan's cornerstone, I shall be Japan's battleship, and I shall never break my oath," he vowed.

The human spirit has a weak side that makes it prone to doubt, fear, and worry. Start a task with a half-hearted attitude, and this weak side will come to the fore, preventing you from attaining your full potential. But if you see your task as a cause, and attack it with a sense of mission, then instead of being dominated by the weaker side of your nature, you will be filled with great strength.

As a leader, you must begin each new task with a sense of mission that will give meaning to your endeavor. As well as having a sense of mission yourself, you must have the ability to impart that same sense to your subordinates, and inspire them with your own enthusiasm. Human beings are partly motivated by hope of reward, but this is not the only motivating force. Greater by far is the joy that comes from carrying out a mission and making sacrifices in the name of a higher cause. Not everyone would agree with Nichiren's approach, but his burning sense of mission is an example to us all.

35

Self-Interrogation

A leader must examine his behavior daily

ZENG SHEN WAS YOUNG enough to be Confucius's grandson, yet he won high praise from the old sage. One of the sayings for which Zeng Shen is famous goes something like this.

"Every day I ask myself three questions. The first is, 'Have I sinned in my thoughts and actions toward others?' The second is, 'Have I broken faith in any of my friendships?' The third is, 'Have I tried to teach anything to others I have not fully learned and understood myself?'"

* * *

If Zeng Shen asked himself these three questions every day, resolving to make no mistakes, then, young as he was, we can well understand why Confucius praised him.

Not only is each of the three questions extremely important in itself, but the practice of examining one's own behavior every day is a habit that every leader should cultivate.

A leader's conduct is very important, since it plays such a critical role in the destiny of nations, and determines the fortunes of so many lives. A leader must resolve to avoid mistakes by regular and rigorous examination of his conscience. Constantly ask yourself whether your policies are correct, and whether you have judged your capabilities correctly. This daily self-examination is something you must never neglect.

Not everything can be clarified by soul-searching alone. When in doubt, ask for a second opinion. Explain your own point of view, then ask for the other person's opinion. By listening to what that person says and thinking it over, you should be able to keep mistakes to a minimum.

Zeng Shen asked himself these three questions every day in order to regulate his own behavior. As leader controlling the welfare of a large number of people, the number of questions you ask yourself should probably be nearer five or even ten.

36

Be Ready to Listen

---

*A leader should always
take into account
what people have to say*

TAKEDA SHINGEN MANAGED TO maintain his domain even
though he was surrounded by enemies. But when
Takeda Katsuyori succeeded him, the domain dissolved
without trace through his foolish actions. The collapse
came about at the battle of Nagashino, at which the
Takeda forces suffered a crushing defeat at the hands of
the united armies of Oda Nobunaga and Tokugawa Ieyasu.

Before the battle began, old vassals of the house of
Takeda, some of whom were reputed to be as wise as
Shingen himself, tried to convince Katsuyori that fighting would be useless. But Katsuyori took no notice,
and finally brought out the Minamoto flag and armor
—treasured family heirloom—in an irrevocable declaration of war.

As a result of Katsuyori's rash action, all of his talented generals, perished in battle, and Takeda Katsuyori himself narrowly escaped with his life. Soon after the Takeda line came to an abrupt end.

* * *

Takeda Katsuyori was said to be a brave warrior and he certainly achieved many great victories in battle. Nevertheless, his miserable fate was surely due to his stubborn refusal to listen to the advice of his vassal. Interestingly, Oda Nobunaga, one of his adversaries, also went against the advice of his old vassals when he won a victory over Imagawa Yoshimoto. But the circumstances on that occasion were quite different. Nobunaga was in a desperate situation requiring a desperate solution. Katsuyori, however, actively sought to engage in battle even though there were other options open to him.

Even a great general should listen to other opinions as much as possible if he is to avoid making mistakes. After all, two heads are better than one. A leader who does not listen can grow stubborn and prone to making errors. He will also alienate people.

On the other hand, a leader who listens attentively and collects information from a wide range of sources is less prone to error, more approachable, and better able to inspire confidence.

Nobunaga, while he could be intractable at times, would seek the opinions of his vassals, especially Hideyoshi. Every leader should be careful to base his actions on a wide range of opinions.

37

Know When to Back Down

---

*A good leader remembers
there is a time to advance and
a time to retreat*

THE FOUNDATIONS OF MODERN Japan were laid more than 100 years ago during the Meiji Restoration. Many died in the course of centralizing power in the hands of the emperor, but it would have been surprising if the emergence of Japan as a modern nation had not been attended by some conflict and sacrifice along the way. In fact, the transition was made relatively smoothly under the circumstances. If it had been less so, the nation might have split into two, leading to a civil war. There was also a danger that Japan might have ended up as a colony of the West. We should be thankful that the worst that happened was some regional infighting.

Broadly speaking, the reason for this relatively pain-less metamorphosis was the force of Japanese tradition. Whether they were aware of it or not, many of Japan's leaders at that time were guided by tradition to act in a way that protected Japan's best interests.

Among the many memorable changes occurring at that time, one of the most remarkable was the return of land, power, and people to the emperor after they had been firmly in the grasp of the Tokugawa shogunate for so long. On the whole, the transfer of executive power, and the transition from feudalism to democracy, was carried out quite peacefully—very unusual in world history.

It could be argued that this was in keeping with the spirit of the age. Nevertheless it was Tokugawa Yoshinobu, then shogun, who had the final say in the matter. Yoshinobu's greatness on this occasion lay in his sacrifice of his own personal interests and the interests of the Tokugawa house to the best interests of Japan as a whole. Assessments of Yoshinobu's career now vary, but I believe his sound judgment on this occasion was a major factor behind the success of the Meiji Restoration.

*   *   *

The ability to advance and retreat as the occasion demands has always been highly regarded, and is just as vital in private life as on the battlefield. This skill is particularly essential for a leader.

But it is by no means easy to conduct oneself correctly in this respect. It is comparatively easy to move forward, but drawing back is more difficult. Nevertheless, a leader who is unable to retreat when the situation calls for it can never be a really great leader. In the battles of old, it was in retreat that the famous generals really showed their mettle. This is a lesson that all leaders would do well to remember.

38

Attention to Detail

**A leader needs
to pay heed to even
the smallest matter**

Iwasaki Yataro, the founder of what was to become
the Mitsubishi Group, once called a senior executive to
his office. "What do you mean by this?" he demanded,
pointing sternly to a piece of paper on his desk. The
manager looked at the paper in surprise, and saw that
it was a leave of absence notice that he himself had
handed in several days before, written on company
notepaper. "How dare you," Iwasaki thundered, "one
of the most senior executives in the company, fail to
make the distinction between public and private business, and use company notepaper to announce that you
are going to take a day off? I must subject you to a
severe penalty."

He then ordered the manager to take a salary cut for
one year. The man realized his mistake, apologized

sincerely, and worked all the harder thereafter.

* * *

Nowadays, most of us would overlook such a small mistake, or, at most, stop at a verbal rebuke and tell the executive to take more care in future. The lesson Iwasaki wanted to teach, however, was that because of their high positions, both of them had to be extremely conscientious. This was the foundation upon which the great Mitsubishi empire was built.

I believe there was also a specific reason why Iwasaki Yataro gave the manager such a large penalty for such a small mistake. As a rule, most people would ensure that the size of the penalty was proportional to the size of the mistake. But consider it another way; it could be said that the really big mistake is the one that occurs despite the fact that the person concerned had thought things through and made a real effort. When someone has made a major mistake, it is more important to stop them worrying about it, encourage them to do better, and find out why the error occurred, so that it won't happen again.

Minor or major, mistakes generally happen because of inattention and complacency on the part of the person who committed them, who often does not realize he has done anything wrong. Just as a massive wooden structure can be undermined by an termite's nest, a small oversight can sow the seed of serious trouble in the future.

We must not become so preoccupied with small details that we lose sight of the larger issues. But a leader should always remember that small mistakes should be severely reprimanded and studied closely, so that they do not grow into large mistakes.

39

Look After Those Who Serve You

A leader should treat people with mercy and keep their welfare at heart

---

HOSHINA MASAYUKI WAS AN eminent lord, famous for restoring the fortunes of the Aizu domain in the seventeenth century. He began by reducing the annual tribute in various ways, including the immediate cancellation of outstanding payments. He also instituted numerous wise governmental measures—anticipating today's welfare policy—which the domain adopted with enthusiasm and flourished.

Masayuki was just one of the many famous lords of the Edo period who treated their subjects with kindness and made every effort to promote their well-being. These lords knew that the people were poor, so reduced the amount they had to contribute to public finances. To compensate, they borrowed from wealthy merchants and other well-off individuals. The yearly tribute was later resumed when the people had regained their prosperity.

There is an earlier example of this. Emperor Nintoku, noticing how thin the smoke coming from his subjects's cooking fires was, realized they were living in poverty so suspended tax and forced service. Three years later, when the smoke was thick again and the people were more prosperous, the emperor reintroduced the tax system.

In those three years, the imperial palace fell into disrepair—the roof started leaking even—but no maintenance work was done. So the story goes, the emperor said, "Heaven created rulers for the sake of the people, and rulers must set the people a good example. If the people are poor, the ruler must live in poverty, and not until the people prosper can the ruler himself live prosperously."

*　　*　　*

The story of the Emperor Nintoku may be just a legend, but it makes the important point that a leader must be kind to his people. Japan has a commendable tradition of producing this kind of leader, and chief among them is Hoshina Masayuki.

Because these leaders treated their people with kindness, their subjects and their domains prospered. The result of mercy was material and spiritual gain.

Even in feudal times, kindness to the people led to prosperity both for the rulers and the ruled. Leaders today must also cultivate the quality of mercy, and give high priority to the well-being of their people.

40

Even-Handedness

A leader must be totally impartial in handing out punishment and rewards

---

WHEN GENERAL MA SUAN of Shu ignored Zhuge Liang's orders in the war against Wei, he blundered badly and the Shu army was forced to retreat.

After the battle, punishment and rewards were meted out according to military practice. Ma Suan's crime in endangering the army was punishable by death. Zhuge Liang had long counted Ma Suan as his mentor, and could not bear the thought of executing him. On the other hand, if he broke with military practice, he would be unable to exert his authority over anyone. Therefore, with tears in his eyes, he had his friend beheaded—a classic example of making a costly sacrifice in the cause of fairness.

Moreover, arguing that he had employed an unsuitable person in an important post by failing to spot this fatal flaw in Ma Suan's character, Zhuge Liang took responsibility for his error and asked to stand down as Shu prime minister. Zhuge Liang's men were so moved by his selfless spirit that the whole army solemnly vowed to attempt another attack on Wei.

* * *

Since olden times, just and unconditional punishment and reward have been recognized as extremely important. Only when great deeds are rewarded, mistakes punished, and justice seen to be done, can the rules of an organization be upheld and its people inspired. If good deeds go unpraised and bad ones unpunished, then people will do just as they please, and law and order will collapse.

Punishment and reward must be meted out without fail, and this must be done appropriately and fairly. Meting out reward or punishment is a very difficult business—too little is ineffective, while too much is counterproductive. It is the good leader who can strike the right balance.

In this you must remember to put aside your personal feelings. If you are influenced by private considerations, you will never be able to achieve the fairness needed to maintain real discipline. Zhuge Liang, who chose to put his beloved friend Ma Suan to death, should be your example.

41

Leave Nothing to Chance

A good leader remembers that the gods help those who help themselves

---

TAKEDA SHINGEN, JAPAN'S FOREMOST warrior of the civil war period, once said, "If someone loses a battle he should not have lost, or when a dynasty perishes that should not have perished, these events are generally attributed to the hand of fate. This is not necessarily so. People often just go about things the wrong way. If they were only more careful in their approach, they would not fail."

*　*　*

All of us, when we meet with any sort of failure, have a tendency to put the blame on bad luck. This has always been so, as evidenced by the existence of proverbs attributing victory or defeat to good or ill fortune.

Takeda Shingen, however, pointed out that this attitude is misguided. He said that all our failures and troubles are our own making. This is a very uncompromising attitude, but for Shingen to have survived in the dog-eat-dog world of the civil war period, such severe self-examination and soul-searching were absolutely necessary.

Things are not much different for the present-day leader. Businessmen, to take just one example, tend to think of profitability as dependent to some extent on luck. While this is true up to a point, I believe that if you adopt a proper attitude toward business, manage your company in a suitable way, and put enough effort into it, then it will be a consistent profit earner as it develops, regardless of the ups and downs of fortune. If your business does not go well, try asking yourself if you have the right attitude to business, or if your management methods are appropriate, or if you are making enough effort. Don't leave your fate in the hands of others until you have done everything possible yourself.

An example from the U.S. space program makes this point. With all preparations for the launch of an Apollo rocket complete, the mission controller murmured, "All we can do now is pray." The implication was that the launch team had done all it could, and now the rest was up to providence. This is what Takeda Shingen was referring to when he mentioned fate. I believe his point was this: before leaving things to providence, we ourselves should do everything that is humanly possible. As a leader, you just cannot afford to sit back and leave things to chance.

42

Exercising Restraint

A leader should know
when to bide his time

WHEN ZHUGE LIANG LED the Shu army against Wei, his opposite number was a man called Sima Zhongda. Like Zhuge Liang, he was a famous warrior, but no match for the former's brilliant tactical skills, and he suffered many a bitter defeat at Zhuge Liang's hands.

Sima Zhongda then changed his approach. He mustered his troops but instead of attacking, carried out flanking maneuvers, and the two armies engaged in a protracted war of nerves. Zhuge Liang sent his troops out in vigorous provocation, but was unable to provoke the Wei army. At length, Zhuge Liang devised a new plan, and sent a present of women's clothing, accompanied by the insulting message: "If you are so reluctant to fight, put these on. If you are man enough to be ashamed, we invite you to join us in battle."

When the Wei warriors heard this, they confronted Sima Zhongda. "We cannot keep silent in the face of such an insult," they cried. "We must engage in battle without delay." Although Sima Zhongda was very angry himself, he kept his temper and persuaded his soldiers to bide their time and not respond to Zhuge Liang's provocation.

In time, Sima Zhongda's tactics paid off. The war of nerves was so protracted that Zhuge Liang eventually fell ill and died, and the Shu army withdrew. Having lost Zhuge Liang, the Shu army later surrendered.

* * *

Bravery is always appealing. We prefer to advance rather than retreat, to ride into battle with flying colors rather than walk away from a fight. Those who do walk away are often reviled and accused of cowardice and unbecoming conduct.

But while it takes courage to fight when the situation calls for it, it takes real courage to avoid a fight and bide one's time. To do this invites contempt rather than praise.

It follows that a leader needs real patience. Unless you can avoid being swayed by personal feelings, unless you can put up with criticism and humiliation, and unless you follow the course you believe to be right, waiting for the appropriate moment, you will never make a really good leader.

"Peace and prosperity are based on forbearance. Anger is the enemy," says Tokugawa Ieyasu in his teachings on the conduct of life. This is a saying that every leader should take to heart.

43

Winning Trust

A leader must be a man of his word

JI BU WAS THE chief minister of Han. He had originally been a general in the Chu army of Xiang Yu, and as such had been a great scourge to the army of Liu Bang, founder of the Han dynasty. But because of a cunning ploy by his chief tactician, Liu Bang went on to soundly defeat Xiang Yu. Afterwards, the victorious commander Liu Bang put a huge price on Ji Bu's head, and declared that any family who sheltered him would be punished for three generations.

In fact, people not only protected Ji Bu but even interceded on his behalf with Liu Bang. This was because Ji Bu always took care to keep his promises, winning such trust and respect that his word alone was said to be worth more than a hundred catties of gold.

Even after he had been pardoned and had sworn

allegiance to the Han dynasty, he retained this outlook and never fawned upon the powerful but was always honest and straightforward. He increasingly won popular trust and steadily rose to high office.

* * *

When you begin an enterprise, trust is very important. If you have people's trust then things will be much easier for you. Trust can be thought of as an invisible force, or an intangible asset.

A leader must win trust. People will shy away from someone they do not trust, whereas they will pledge their allegiance to someone they do.

Trust, however, is not something you acquire overnight. It can take years to cultivate a reputation for reliability. On the other hand, trust is easily lost. Even if you have built up trust by many years of honest toil, a single lie can destroy the reputation you have so painstakingly won.

In the past, a distinguished family or a long-established business could make a small mistake without forfeiting the trust placed in it, because the strength of the trust built up over the years would work in its favor. Now, though, news travels fast. Even a small slip-up can be fatal. To maintain and cultivate trust, a leader must take every precaution to ensure that mistakes do not occur.

44

Believe in Your Staff

A leader must trust his subordinates to get the best out of them

---

LIU BANG, FOUNDER OF the Han dynasty, first had to fight Xiang Yu for supremacy. Xiang Yu initially made the stronger showing, and Liu Bang's forces were hard pressed. But Liu Bang had a resourceful general who developed a clever ploy to convince Xiang Yu that his tactician, Fan Zeng, and his most senior officers were secretly in league with the enemy. Xiang Yu was completely taken in and began to doubt Fan Zeng, who resented this and became thoroughly alienated. In the end, Xiang Yu, who had enjoyed the early ascendancy, gradually lost the initiative and was completely routed. Afterwards, Liu Bang explained Xiang Yu's defeat as follows: "I made the best use of my subordinates; Xiang Yu didn't even know how to use Fan Zeng properly."

* * *

There are many tricks to the art of using people, but the most important is to trust them and delegate work to them. This pleases subordinates, and it is also the only way to instill in them a sense of responsibility. A person who has been entrusted with a task will use his own resources and make his best efforts to carry it out. People only give of their best when they are trusted.

Admittedly, giving people your complete trust is easier said than done. Doubts creep in—"Can that person really cope with this?" "This information is highly confidential; if I tell that person, mightn't he disclose it to someone else?" It is certainly true that no one is 100-percent reliable. Nevertheless, in a crisis or a delicate situation, people will only trust you if their trust is reciprocated. If you cannot conquer your doubt, and have to make a pretense of trusting people by going through the motions of delegating work, you will not be able to create good working relationships with your subordinates.

First and foremost, therefore, you must aim to create a basic bond of trust with people. As long as this exists, then people will accept that your motives are good and keep their faith in you, even if occasions arise when their faith was actually unjustified.

The modern world is plagued by distrust on many fronts. This gives rise to strife and stress, and in its most extreme manifestations, can lead to physical destruction. This makes it all the more important that leaders everywhere should base their dealings with people on a sense of trust.

45

Love What You Do

If a leader does not enjoy his work, he is unfit for the job

ALMOST 200 YEARS AFTER THE foundation of the great Han empire, the government lapsed into chaos, eventually disintegrating completely. The country seemed once more headed for civil war until a hero emerged on the scene and rescued it from disaster. The man of the hour, who rapidly quelled the disorder and restored the sovereignty of the Han, was the emperor known as Guang Wu Di. An outstanding warrior, Wu Di was also famous for his skills in government. Passionately absorbed in the affairs of state, he worked from early in the morning until late in the evening, sometimes staying up half the night studying or in conference with his retainers. The crown prince, who feared for Wu Di's health, tried to persuade him to moderate his schedule, but Wu Di replied, "There is no need to be concerned.

I enjoy my work, so no matter how much I do, I never get tired."

* * *

"Love what you do and you'll become good at it," goes the old proverb. Whatever your work, it is vitally important that you love it. Unless you love your work, then no matter how long you toil, you will find it difficult to succeed. Craftsmen and sports champions can put up with harsh training and gruelling practice only because they love their art or their sport. Even with this passion, excellence and success are not easily achieved. Without it, there is no chance at all.

This goes for leaders, too. It is vitally important that you love your work as a leader. If you are a politician, you must love politics. If you are a manager, you must love management.

On the whole, a leader's lot is not a happy one. Using people always brings problems and worries. All is well when everyone listens attentively to what you have to say, and does exactly what you ask of them. Not everyone will do this, however. Some people will complain, while others may disregard your orders. This alone is enough to wear you out. Moreover, problems come up one after another, and it is no easy task to find the right solution to each one.

Anyone who is daunted and dismayed by such things will never make a leader. A leader must love his work, no matter how difficult it seems to others.

46

Everyone Has a Role to Play

A good leader finds a use for everyone

AMONG HORI HIDEMASA'S RETAINERS was a man whose facial expression made him look as if he were in perpetual mourning. His eyes were always brimming with tears, his brow was always furrowed, and he always looked sad. The other retainers begged Hidemasa to get rid of him. "That man has such an unpleasant expression—he's a real eyesore!" they said. "People laugh at you for employing such an ugly retainer. Why not be done with him?"

"What you say is true," Hidemasa replied, "but there is no one better able to lead memorial services and carry messages of condolence. Everyone has their uses, and a great house such as this must employ all manner of people."

*   *   *

No two faces are exactly alike, and no two people are exactly the same. Consider the character, temperament, abilities, and way of thinking of the individuals you encounter and you will find that they are all different. In fact, the combinations are infinite. Nobody is good at everything, and nobody is bad at everything. Everyone has his good points and bad points, his strengths and weaknesses.

It is very important for a leader to be able to size up the qualities of his subordinates, to use their strengths while accepting their weaknesses, and so make the most of them.

This, too, is easier said than done. There is a natural tendency to focus on a narrow range of abilities and judge people as useful if they shine in this area, and as useless if they do not.

Living in the civil war period, Hori Hidemasa's retainers gave top priority to bravery, and so they saw the sad-faced man as being useless to their lord. But even in time of war, fighting is not the only business. All sorts of people—not just heroes—have a part to play. Hidemasa was aware of this, and this is why he said that a great house needs to employ all manner of people.

Modern society is so complex that it cannot be compared with society in Hidemasa's day, but the saying, "It takes all sorts to make a world" is truer than ever. Today's leaders must take even more care than Hidemasa to employ a wide variety of people. Nobody is perfect, but nobody is entirely useless, either. Bear this in mind and make the best use of everyone under your command.

47

A Matter of Principle

A steadfast leader will always command respect

In 1595, a great earthquake in Kyoto killed many people and destroyed Toyotomi Hideyoshi's castle at Fushimi. Kato Kiyomasa was under house arrest at the time for incurring Hideyoshi's displeasure, but he immediately hastened to the scene with his retainers to offer his help. "Even if I am to be punished later, I cannot stand by idly at such a time," he said. The ingenuous loyalty that inspired this action so pleased Hideyoshi that he forgave Kiyomasa and reinstated him as his right-hand man.

Another of the many stories that illustrate Kato Kiyomasa's commitment to his principles goes as follows. When Hideyoshi died, all his followers but Kiyomasa switched their allegiance to Tokugawa Ieyasu. Kiyomasa, however, protected Hideyoshi's heir, Hideyori, and risked his life to attend the negotiations between Ieyasu and Hideyori at Nijo Castle in Kyoto. Kiyomasa never forgot Hideyoshi's favor, and did his utmost to preserve the safety of the Toyotomi family. Even Ieyasu was forced to admire his steadfastness.

* * *

A man of principle will always show his true colors in the end. Hence he will always have a clear conscience. If his conscience is clear, he will be free of worries and fears, and will always live an open, honest life. If a man merely presents a veneer of honesty, he will have to be constantly on his guard in order to maintain this facade. This in itself will weigh on his conscience, making him incapable of functioning with true conviction.

This is equally true in business and politics. Business is often seen as a game of strategy in which some tactical skills are required. But if you are unable to make a clean breast of things when the occasion demands it, you will also be unable to build up a relationship of true understanding with your business associates. If you work entirely by tactics and intrigue, you will not be able to cultivate the confidence of your associates in the long term.

This applies to politics, too: in the end, you need to explain the facts frankly. If you flatter people and tell them only what they want to hear, you may win temporary popularity, but you will not be able to help your people when they most need it. A leader must be aware that, in the final analysis, it is his straightforward commitment to principle that moves people.

48

The Ultimate Sacrifice

*A leader must be
prepared to give his life
for his people and his cause*

DURING ONE OF TOYOTOMI Hideyoshi's battles with the
Mori family, he isolated Takamatsu Castle by diverting
the flow of a nearby river. Inside the castle, the Mori
garrison found itself cut off from reinforcements by the
flood and rapidly running short of food. In the face of
what seemed like certain doom, it began to lose heart.

It was then that Shimizu Muneharu, the Mori commander, announced that he would give up his own life
to save the lives of his soldiers. In return, Hideyoshi's
army made an offer of peace. Muneharu then rowed
out into the waters surrounding the castle, and, in full
view of both armies, voluntarily took his life by committing harakiri.

* * *

It is often said that thousands die to raise one hero to victory, but the other side of the coin is that a hero's death can save a thousand lives. The above story, like many others, shows that the warriors of the civil war period were quite prepared to sacrifice themselves in order to save the lives of those under their command.

This sense of responsibility motivated great generals such as Muneharu, who, when all hope of victory was gone, took the responsibility on himself and gave his own life to save the lives of his men.

Today's leaders need exactly the same sense of responsibility, although there should be no question of committing harakiri. Nevertheless, it is just as imperative that, when faced with an emergency, a leader is prepared to risk his own life and take all responsibility on himself. If you are the leader of a nation, you must be prepared to die for your people. If you are the president of a company, you must be prepared to die for your employees. If you are the head of a division or section, you must be prepared to die for your subordinates. If you have this sense of responsibility, then your subordinates will rally round, and will bring their collective strength to bear on the problem. A leader who does not have this strong sense of responsibility will never be able to make proper use of his work force.

49

Vox Populi

A leader must assume that public opinion is generally correct

KURODA YOSHITAKA WAS A tactician who rose to great power with Toyotomi Hideyoshi as the latter became supreme ruler of Japan. He is said to have made the following remark.

"I fear my lord's wrath more than the wrath of heaven, but I fear the wrath of the people most of all. Heaven's reprisal can be averted by prayer, and my lord's wrath can be averted by apologizing and pleading for his forgiveness. But once you offend the people, prayers and apologies are useless, and you will definitely lose your entire realm. The wrath of the people is the most frightening thing in the world."

* * *

The world is made up of sorts of people. Everyone has his own way of thinking and his own way of judging right and wrong. Some people judge well, and some do not. But if you take public opinion as a whole, it generally discerns the truth of things.

If you do the right thing, your action will meet with public acceptance: if you do the wrong thing, your action will meet with public rejection. Once you lose the public's trust, it is terribly difficult to win back favor.

If you incur the wrath of a single lord, his anger may be fierce, and heads may roll, but because he is just one man, it is at least possible to avert his anger by apologizing or having someone intercede for you.

But if you incur the wrath of the whole populace, apologizing will not do any good. Hence you must fear the wrath of the populace more than anything else.

A Latin proverb puts it thus—*vox populi, vox dei*. Or as the great American President Abraham Lincoln said: "You can fool all the people some of the time, and some of the people all the time, but you can't fool all the people all of the time."

In short, you must listen to the voice of the people as if it were the voice of God, and obey it honestly and sincerely. As long as you do this, the world will receive you warmly, and will have no reason to rise in anger. It is a leader who strays from this path that incurs the wrath of the people.

Kuroda Yoshitaka was a wise leader on a par with Zhang Liang, the great tactician of ancient China. Although Kuroda is often portrayed as a Machiavellian figure, his sound grasp of this point is a lesson for every leader.

50

The Power of Persuasion

A good leader knows how to win people to his cause

IN THE LATTER HALF of the nineteenth century, plans were being made to lay railroads in Japan, but many in the new Meiji government were deeply entrenched in the old ways of thinking, and strongly opposed the project. Iwakura Tomomi, a court noble, persuaded the doubters with the following speech.

"We have now moved the capital from Kyoto to Tokyo. But the graves of the imperial family for the past 1,000 years and more have been in Kyoto, so the emperor will have to make regular visits to Kyoto. If the imperial party must travel by road this will surely cause great difficulties. But if the emperor were able to travel by locomotive, such difficulties could be averted. Our filial piety to the emperor makes it necessary for us to support the railroads."

Upon hearing this, those who had previously opposed the railroads conceded the logic of the argument and unanimously agreed that laying of tracks should go ahead.

*   *   *

As a leader, whenever you begin a major project, you will naturally have to employ and motivate large numbers of people. It is vital that these people share your way of thinking and agree with you.

To be able to persuade people, it goes without saying that your fundamental ethos and approach must be correct. If they are not, you will find it very difficult to motivate people. Even if your idea or proposal is a good one, it does not necessarily follow that people will adopt it and see eye to eye with you. If you get carried away with your ideas and try to force your opinions on people, rather than persuading them, you will have the opposite effect of encouraging them to oppose you.

When you explain your ideas, the way you state your case is very important. You will only be able to do so convincingly if you take into account the time, the place, and the audience. You must give full consideration to winning the hearts and minds of the people you are trying to persuade.

A leader who lacks the power of persuasion will have a hard time leading and motivating those under his command. Iwakura Tomomi's persuasive technique is a lesson for all leaders.

51

Going Against the Flow

A leader must recognize when to follow that flash of inspiration that transcends common sense

---

SOME 40,000 TROOPS COMMANDED BY Imagawa Yoshimoto were bearing down on Oda Nobunaga's stronghold. All Nobunaga's senior statesmen were in favor of staying put and withstanding the siege, arguing that since the forces at their disposal numbered barely 3,000, they stood little chance of success if they launched a counter-attack.

Nobunaga, however, disregarding the opinion of his senior statesmen, decided to leave the castle and fight. He sent out a single horseman to spearhead the attack and went on to win a miraculous victory.

* * *

An army cooped up inside a castle can still put up

some sort of fight. But outnumbered ten to one by the enemy, and cut off from its allies, Nobunaga's army could not have resisted for long, and defeat would have been inevitable. Under these circumstances, there were two choices: to sit and wait for death or risk everything in a desperate bid for victory. Even though the chance of success was slight, Nobunaga gambled and succeeded brilliantly.

In most circumstances, it is appropriate that a leader listen carefully to the opinion of the majority. If he persists in following his own judgment, regardless of the generally-held view, he risks becoming intransigent and prone to making mistakes. Public opinion is a very useful guideline to help keep a leader from erring.

This principle, however, applies mainly to ordinary situations; in extraordinary situations, it is not always adequate. The generally-held view is largely a matter of common sense based on past experience. Now common sense, or the received view, is generally the product of a collective wisdom, and is thus a valuable thing, but circumstances out of the ordinary require a new inspiration, a fresh approach, that oversteps the boundaries of common sense.

On these occasions, a leader must rise above public opinion, and dream up a more inspired approach. In other words, he must dare to ignore public opinion, even to fly in its face, but only in the most unusual circumstances. This is exactly what Oda Nobunaga did. If he had gone along with the generally-held view, he would not have won a victory. In rising above public opinion, he showed his greatness as a leader.

52

In Touch with Tomorrow

---

*A leader must have
the ability to act with foresight*

DURING JAPAN'S CIVIL WAR period, there was widespread rivalry between feudal houses. The strongest of these was the Takeda family, backed by its fearless cavalry. Trained by Takeda Shingen, the famous general, the cavalry was the scourge of neighboring provinces, and his troops had never known defeat. The house's strength remained undiminished when Takeda Shingen died and his son, Katsuyori, became head of the family. Subsequently, however, the Takeda forces suffered total defeat at the hands of the combined armies of Oda Nobunaga and Tokugawa Ieyasu at the battle of Naga-shino in 1575, which marked the beginning of the Takeda house's decline and fall.

Nobunaga's strategy at the battle of Nagashino was as follows. Using 5,000 firearms divided up into three groups, he kept up a constant barrage of fire. He also drove large numbers of stakes into the ground in front of his army, and stretched ropes between them. The horses of Takeda's cavalry got their legs entangled in these ropes, whereupon Oda Nobunaga's troops fired on them in volleys. It was more of turkey shoot than a battle. Takeda's army suffered huge casualties and was comprehensively beaten.

* * *

Oda Nobunaga won this victory not because he was a stronger general or had better soldiers, but because he was using weapons of a completely different nature to Takeda's. He realized that the age of firearms had arrived, and made his preparations long before the fighting began. However strong Takeda's cavalry was, it could never have won, because it was shot to pieces before it reached the enemy line. In the final analysis, victory was Nobunaga's before the fighting began.

The sort of foresight displayed by Nobunaga is extremely important in a leader. A leader who lacks foresight is not qualified for the position. Circumstances quickly change: what is in use today may be obsolete tomorrow. As a leader, you must keep an eye on the way the times are changing, so that you can predict the shape of things to come and prepare accordingly. Only this way can you safeguard the peace and security of your nation—or the future prospects of your company. To find yourself suddenly confronted with a new situation, then to have to search hurriedly for a solution, is no recipe for success.

Looking back over history, it seems to me that whenever a country enjoys a period of prosperity, this is almost invariably due to the foresight of its leaders.

53

Stay One Step Ahead

**A leader must be
able to think and act faster than
his employees**

ONE DAY, AS THE Chinese Emperor Yao was making his
way to the city, he heard an old peasant farmer singing
this song.

*Rise at dawn, rest at sundown,
Dig a well for water, plow a field for rice;
What use is the emperor to us?*

To Yao, this was ample proof that his government was
doing its job properly, and he rejoiced.

* * *

In practice, of course, most people only become
interested in politics and conscious of their rulers when

normal life is disrupted at times of political unrest. Yao's greatness as emperor was his ability to create a stable climate in which his subjects toiled and were content. The farmer was devoted to his work and had no worries about anything else. He enjoyed life. He was blissfully unaware that this state of affairs was only possible because the government was functioning correctly.

It is just as important today as it was then that people should be able to go about their business in peace. All leaders should work toward this goal.

To achieve this, a leader must concern himself with the future of the country before the people begin to do so. A leader must be the first to worry, and in a wider sense, he has a duty to think things out before everyone else does, to come up with new ideas, and to take appropriate action.

Naturally, a leader needs to be able to handle a crisis, but it is even more important that he should have the foresight to prevent crises occurring in the first place. The modern business manager, to take one example, needs to think and act more quickly than his employees. A leader who does not have the sense of responsibility to act in this way should step down at once.

54

Don't Delay

A leader must act
promptly in a crisis

TOYOTOMI HIDEYOSHI WAS FIGHTING Shibata Katsuie. One day, when Hideyoshi and his troops left camp, Shibata Katsuie's general, Sakuma Morimasa, seized the opportunity to take the camp by surprise. Capturing the fort brought significant military advantage, but when Hideyoshi heard the news he immediately mobilized his entire army and returned at speed. He and his men marched more than 50 kilometers in barely half a day, routing the enemy, who were panicked by Hideyoshi's rapid return. Heartened by its success, Hideyoshi's army mounted an attack on Morimasa's main camp, and won a decisive victory.

Hideyoshi had already engaged and crushed the forces of Akechi Mitsuhide at the battle of Yamazaki only eleven days after Mitsuhide had treacherously assassinated Oda Nobunaga. This was all the more remarkable since at the time of the assassination Hideyoshi had been confronting his arch rival Mori in an armed stand-off. It is testimony to his leadership skills that he was able to triumph again and again.

* * *

Given that Hideyoshi was travelling on foot, his actions were extremely rapid. In fact, it is said that neither Mitsuhide, nor any of Nobunaga's retainers and allies, had thought that Hideyoshi could react so quickly.

This ability to act faster than anyone expected brought him many victories, and was one of the main reasons why he was able to gain control of Japan.

It has long been said that "prompt action is the secret of warfare." Another saying goes, "First come, first served." In some cases, promptness in grasping a momentary advantage is the difference between victory and defeat: hesitate, and the opportunity is lost. For a military leader, decisiveness and prompt action are vital.

This is just as relevant to the running of a country or a corporation as it is to the prosecution of warfare. In both politics and business, circumstances can change completely from one minute to the next: a day's delay can lead to a year's delay. A leader must never put off making decisions or acting on them.

Of course, some things need to be managed very cautiously, requiring careful consideration and consultation with others before a decision is taken. But it is absolutely vital that a leader be capable of prompt decisions and prompt actions in times of crisis.

55

Practice What You Preach

*A leader should lead
by example*

To PERCEIVE THE TRUTH is to make it impossible not to
act in accordance with it, the philosopher Socrates
believed. The government sentenced him to death for
what it regarded as his highly dangerous views.

Before the sentence was carried out, friends went to
visit Socrates in jail. They urged him to escape, and
even devised a plan. Socrates firmly rejected this sug-
gestion. "All my life I have told people to obey the law
of the land," he said. "If the law is wrong or inappropri-
ate, then we should revise it by discussion, but as long
as it is the law of the land, we must obey it. This is what
I have always preached, and although I am a victim of
injustice, I cannot go against my own precepts for fear
of death. A man's first priority is not just to live, but to
lead a good and just life." He then calmly drank the

deadly poison mandated by the death penalty.

* * *

Great truths must be disseminated. It is also important to act on them and provide a good example. If you preach a great truth, but fail to practice it in your own life, you will never convince anyone.

I think we may describe Socrates, Buddha, Christ, and Confucius as the world's great sages. This is because, as well as teaching great truths, they practiced what they preached, even to the extent of giving up their lives. In Socrates' case, by dying he enshrined his philosophy as an eternal truth. The fact that he was prepared to die for his beliefs moved the hearts of the people, and inspired their infinite respect.

As a leader, you must convey your principles to people, but you yourself must set the example. Human nature being what it is, you may not always be able to live up to your principles 100 percent. Nevertheless, a leader who lacks the courage to practice what he preaches must realize that he will never be able to command the whole-hearted loyalty of those around him.

56

Fight for the Right Reasons

A leader should make it clear why his cause is a just one

ASAI NAGAMASA MARRIED THE younger sister of Oda Nobunaga, and enjoyed the full confidence of his brother-in-law for many years. But when Oda Nobunaga attacked the house of Asakura, long on friendly terms with the house of Asai, Nagamasa immediately mobilized his troops and mounted an attack on the rear of Nobunaga's army. Nobunaga was hard pressed, and only just managed to return to Kyoto safely.

Some of Nagamasa's retainers tried to dissuade him from attacking Nobunaga head on. Not only was Nobunaga was a relative by marriage, they argued, but more important, he was aligned with the imperial court, fighting for the great cause of national unity. Nagamasa, his retainers pointed out, was fighting for essentially personal reasons.

If he really could not bear to give up his friendship with the house of Asakura, they advised him, the best thing would be to persuade the Asakura to join him and fight for Nobunaga's great cause. Nagamasa, however, would not listen and went on to confront Nobunaga, which eventually led to his own downfall.

* * *

Asai Nagamasa was a great warrior, who always fought a fair fight, and died an honorable death. Nevertheless, his house perished, isolated from its neighbors, principally because his cause was misguided. Oda Nobunaga, on the other hand, had always proclaimed that his aim was to unite the war-torn country and restore peace under the traditional sovereignty of the imperial family. This argument won the hearts of a war-weary people, and inspired his followers with a sense of mission which motivated them to give of their best.

Many leaders go to great lengths to make clear the justice of their cause before entering battle. These men made it plain that they are not fighting for their own personal advancement but for the general good. With this rallying cry they rally support and inspire those under their command.

No matter how large your army, you will fail to win support if you lack a just cause; in the long run, you will accomplish nothing. The relevance of this truth is not limited to the battlefield. The expression "in a good cause" may sound a little old-fashioned, but it is equally vital in business management and in politics. As a leader, you must be clear about your goals and make them clear to everyone under your command.

57

The Big Picture

A leader's role is to focus on the fundamentals

As a young man, Ikeda Mitsumasa went to visit Itakura Katsushige, the famous shogunal deputy in Kyoto, to ask his advice on government. "Good government is like keeping miso bean paste in a square container, and scooping it out with a round ladle," said Katsushige.

"But you can't scoop the corners!" Mitsumasa protested. "That's the whole point," Katsushige replied. "You are a wise man who will approach the task of government with enthusiasm. If you pay too much attention to detail, however, the country will not prosper."

*   *   *

This was good advice for an idealistic young lord to

receive from a veteran politician who had a keen insight into human nature.

Of course, a leader shouldn't neglect small detail. As the proverb goes, "Even the biggest of houses can be toppled by a nest of termites." Hence the president of a company may sometimes need to scold a subordinate for wasting a sheet of paper. On the other hand, if that same president oversees every little task, his employees will grow too uncomfortable to have any enthusiasm for their work. Anyway, in a large company, it is not possible for the president to chase after every detail.

This also applies to the government of a country. If the government passes laws on everything, and binds people in a tight web of rules and regulations, the country will not function properly. Citizens will feel constricted and oppressed, and their vitality will be undermined.

Hence although small details must not be neglected, a leader should also avoid becoming preoccupied with minor details and losing sight of the wood for the trees. As a leader, you must keep a firm grip on the fundamental issues, and leave your subordinates to take care of the rest. In the end, this will help them develop a healthy self-discipline and a positive attitude to their work.

58

At the Heart of Things

---

*A leader should stay at
headquarters and let his subordinates
go out in the field*

MINAMOTO YORITOMO MANAGED TO destroy the Heike at
Fujigawa almost without a fight. Then he mustered his
troops and set off for Kyoto. But some of his ministers
advised him to consolidate his base nearer to home.
Yoritomo accepted this advice and brought his soldiers
back. Henceforth, he himself stayed mainly in Kamakura, where he set up the Kamakura shogunate, Japan's first military government, dispatching his brothers Noriyori and Yoshitsune and his generals to do
his fighting for him.

* * *

A few years after I started my own business, a
Buddhist monk gave me the following advice. "The

boss should stay at home, the clerks should go out." At the time, I gave this little thought, but later, as I became more experienced, I realized that his words contained a deeper lesson.

In fact, the question of whether the boss should stay at head office, or go out and lead the action, is a very difficult one, and one to which it is hard to give a definitive answer.

In some situations, the commander needs to take the initiative and fight at the front line. As a general rule, however, I believe that things do go more smoothly if the leader stays put and sends his subordinates to handle outside matters. China's great leader Mao Zedong is said to have traveled overseas once, as a young man, but after that he never left China. It was Prime Minister Zhou Enlai and his ministers who went abroad on China's behalf.

Nowadays, we have all sorts of modern conveniences. The president of a company can stay at head office and still be in close touch with subsidiaries and branch offices all over the world. A leader must be prepared to go to the front line in a crisis, but, as a general rule, he should stay at home and let his subordinates take care of external affairs.

59

Calling the Shots

A leader must always be in control

WHEN MAEDA TOSHIIE HEARD that one of the castles in his domain had been surrounded by the army of Sassa Narimasa, he immediately prepared to go to the front to lead a counterattack. Then one of his retainers told him about a hermit monk who was skilled at fortune-telling, and he advised him to consult the monk about the prospects for that day. Toshiie consented, but after the monk arrived, had prepared his scrolls, and was about to cast the divining rods, Toshiie said to him, "I have already made up my mind to attack, whatever fate may decree, so please bear this in mind when you tell my fortune." The monk immediately put away his scrolls, saying, "Today is the best day and now is the best time." Toshiie laughed and said, "You truly are an expert fortune-teller." He then mounted a ferocious attack and scored a resounding victory.

* * *

This story shows a great general behaving just as he ought to behave. It is very important for a leader to listen to those under his command. In some situations, it may be a good idea to use a mystical power to raise morale, just as Maeda Toshiie did by summoning the fortune-teller. Whatever the situation, however, the leader must be quite clear about what he intends to do.

Remember that if you do not have a plan of your own, and rely entirely on other people's opinions and mystic portents, then you are no leader.

In the past, a feudal lord would, as a rule, employ a tactician, and many lords owed their military success to their tactician's advice. But crucially, the lord always had the final say. He was not obliged to do as his tactician advised him. It could be argued that it was no use having a tactician if his advice was not followed, but I would disagree: the function of the tactician was to give the lord a more complete view of the possibilities so that he could make better decisions.

By definition, a leader should always be independent, and lead from the front. You must make sure that you have complete control of the situation before listening to the opinions of others or making use of mystical powers: only then can you truly use these supports to best advantage.

60

The Greater Good

A leader must look beyond small differences of opinion

THE CLIMAX OF THE Meiji Restoration, which represented the dramatic birth of modern Japan, was undeniably the bloodless capitulation of Edo in 1868. If the opposing factions had gone to war, this would have led to incalculable bloodshed, and Japan would never have evolved into an economic superpower.

The leading figures in this drama were Katsu Kaishu, chief negotiator for the Tokugawa shogunate, and Saigo Takamori, representing the pro-imperial forces. It was extremely fortunate for Japan that these two great men, who respected and trusted one another, were the nation's leaders at its moment of crisis.

At the time, many people on both sides were in favor of a military showdown. There were equal prospects for victory, and if it came to an actual war, there was no knowing who would win. Further complicating the matter, Britain was backing pro-imperialist forces, while France was supporting the shogunate armies.

If the imperial forces had thought only of establishing their own authority, and if the shogunate had thought only of its own future, negotiations would have broken down, and both sides would have been overwhelmed by the influence of strong foreign powers.

But both Katsu Kaishu and Saigo Takamori were aware of the broader issues, and saw Japan's future as their top priority. At that time, one Asian country after another was being colonized by the Western powers. If Japan had succumbed to civil war, then no matter which side won, the country would have fallen into chaos, making it vulnerable to foreign intervention and paving the way for ruin. This had to be avoided at all costs, so the two men decided to put aside their minor differences for the common cause. Their agreement made the bloodless capitulation of Edo possible.

Of course, they were not the only ones who thought like this: many informed people at that time held the same views. This allowed the Meiji Restoration to proceed comparatively smoothly, despite a few complications and some conflict, culminating in the successful emergence of modern Japan.

*　*　*

As a leader, you should avoid becoming over-preoccupied with immediate concerns and minor details, and take the long view instead. Never stop asking yourself what the important issues are, and always aim to do the right thing. Try to see the whole situation in perspective, and be willing to disregard small differences for the common cause.

61

Do What You Know to Be Right

A leader needs the courage of his convictions

DURING U.S. PRESIDENT JOHN F. Kennedy's term of office, the Soviet Union set up a missile base in Cuba, which the United States only found out about when the base was near completion. Kennedy sent a communique to the Soviet leader, Nikita Khrushchev, notifying him of the American people's severe disquiet at the setting up of a Soviet missile base so close to the United States and asking him to remove it. The communique contained the stern ultimatum that if the Soviet Union did not remove the base by a certain date, the United States would do so. Kennedy was prepared to engage in war if necessary, and he mobilized the fleet and set up a naval blockade in preparation for battle. In the face of U.S. determination, Khrushchev eventually agreed to remove the base.

* * *

President Kennedy succeeded because he was determined. This determination, I believe, derived from deciding on the right course of action and then having the conviction to carry it out. He knew that if a missile base were set up in Cuba, the security of the United States would be deeply compromised. This was something he could not allow at any cost. This knowledge gave him the determination to resort to arms if the need arose. His determination naturally made an impression on Khrushchev, and his actions had the desired effect.

Of course, it goes without saying that U.S. military strength added weight to Kennedy's ultimatum. Without this, his demand for the removal of the missile base would have been ignored. But given the Soviet Union's own considerable military capabilities at the time, it would not have bowed to U.S. pressure on the strength of the military considerations alone. Military force only counts for something when backed up by firm conviction. Without it, strength does not always prevail. It is thus vital for a leader to have the courage of his convictions if he is to be successful.

62

Something in Reserve

*A leader must have
resources to call upon
in emergencies*

WHEN UESUGI HARUNORI INHERITED the extensive Yone-
zawa domain at the age of seventeen, the domain was
in severe financial straits. It had experienced a disas-
trous famine in which many people died, and there
were no funds available to help survivors.

Harunori began by cutting expenses. He announced
tough austerity measures, and selected a man of ability
to take charge of increasing agricultural output. He also
made provision for future emergencies. As a result,
warehouses were full for the next ten years, and even
when a volcanic eruption caused another famine, the
domain was able to tide itself over without a repetition
of the terrible disaster of the past. Although it had
accumulated huge debts, the domain's finances gradually became much healthier as the productivity drive

bore fruit. Harunori was long remembered as one of the most able lords of the Edo period and many famous lords followed his example.

* * *

This is what I call reservoir management. A reservoir is created by damming a river where water is plentiful. The water can then be discharged at regular intervals in time of drought, and used for power generation and for irrigation. This principle can be equally well applied to the running of a country, an industry, or a company— or indeed to any area of human endeavor. Using the reservoir principle, you can achieve steady, stable development unaffected by short-term fluctuations in business. Every leader should bear this management approach in mind.

Simply put, reservoir management is the art of leaving a margin. In business, for example, this would mean procuring 110 units of capital when only 100 are needed: the extra 10 units represent a reservoir of capital. In running an industrial plant, the reservoir principle may be applied by designing the plant to operate comfortably at 90 percent capacity: a sudden increase in demand can then be accommodated without great trouble, using the 10 percent margin. Reservoir management means you should maintain a minimum level of stock. This way, you ensure that your operations run smoothly and are not disrupted by short-term fluctuations.

Reservoir management is equally important in the running of nations, self-governing bodies, and all types of organizations. As a first step, create a spiritual reservoir in your own heart for when an unexpected emergency tests you.

63

The Human Factor

A leader must believe in the brotherhood of man

THE EMPEROR MEIJI WROTE a famous poem that goes something like this:

On all four seas
I thought all men were brothers,
Yet in this world
Why do winds and waves
Now rise and stir?

The emperor composed this poem in 1904, the year that the Russo-Japanese war began. The fact that the emperor wrote these words at a time when the two countries were engaged in hostilities must have made a deep impression on his subjects.

The emperor felt no hatred for the Russian people.

Unfortunate circumstances, he believed, had forced Japan and Russia to become enemies and join battle, whereas the people of both nations should actually be living in harmony and mutual prosperity, as brothers.

This sentiment was not confined to the Emperor Meiji, but was an expression of traditional Japanese spirit, and, on a wider scale, would have been a desire shared by most Japanese.

*　　*　　*

Let us turn our attention to the world as it is today. It cannot be denied that much of what occurs is incompatible with this desire for harmony and shared prosperity. The main reason for this is that the modern world has forgotten that all men are brothers.

This makes it more vital than ever that leaders should believe in the brotherhood of man and behave accordingly. If all leaders took this concept to heart and acted on it, there would be very little conflict in the world. Excessive economic competition would disappear, and managers and workers would no longer lock horns in conflict. Political parties would refrain from needless opposition, and would devote their energies to the welfare of the nation. War, the greatest cause of misery, would gradually disappear from the face of the earth.

Of course, despite the Emperor Meiji's private feelings, two major wars occurred during his reign, so it cannot really be said that he created conditions of harmony and mutual prosperity. Nevertheless, the philosophy that all men are brothers is one to which every leader should subscribe.

64

Who Chooses Who?

---

*A leader must be
accepted by his subordinates
if he is to succeed*

Hojo Ujiyasu was one of the great warlords of the civil
war period. But as well as being a famous general with
a reputation for invincibility he was also a good ruler,
and just as skilled with the pen as he was with the
sword.

When Hojo Ujiyasu stepped down, leadership of the
family passed to his son Ujimasa. What did he look
forward to doing, he asked his son, now that he was in
charge? "I look forward to choosing my men and judging their abilities," Ujimasa replied.

"That is good," said Ujiyasu, "but remember this: it
is usually the leader who chooses his subordinates, but
on occasion, it is the subordinates who choose their
leader. Treat your subordinates well from day to day,
and show your people mercy. If you don't, then in time

of crisis, they will look elsewhere for leadership. If you would be leader, always bear this in mind. This is not always obvious to someone born to a rich family who has never wanted for anything. You must take good care in this respect."

* * *

At first glance, it appears that it is the leader who uses his subordinates to do his work. But it can also be argued that the leader is the one who is used. Hence, even when giving orders to subordinates, remember that they are doing you a favor by carrying out your wishes. Any leader who rejects this point of view, and believes that people can be made to do things simply by issuing commands, is sadly mistaken. Only when a leader possesses humility will he be chosen by his subordinates to lead them. The larger the group or organization, the more important it is that the leader should possess humility.

65

The Right Man for the Job

A leader must be objective in matters of personnel

YOSHIMUNE, THE EIGHTH TOKUGAWA shogun, was famous for having brought order to a troubled society by initiating wise reforms. So successful was he in reinstating the power and authority of the regime that he was referred to as a second Ieyasu, the original founder of the Tokugawa shogunate. Yoshimune was a great believer in employing the best man for the job. One of the men he appointed was Ooka Tadasuke, the magistrate of Edo and a man noted for the fairness and justice of his deliberations.

Yoshimune's predecessors had an undeniable tendency to give important positions to their favorite retainers, whereas Yoshimune appointed Ooka Tadasuke and many other men on the strength of their character and ability. In feudal times, Yoshimune's system of appointment based on merit was a great innovation, and it resulted in a very effective government.

*　*　*

People have different talents and abilities. Giving an individual the right job allows him to put his special abilities to best use. Such a policy gets the most out of a person and makes him happy, but that is not all: when an individual is in the right job, he carries out his duties more effectively. This in turn helps other individuals to do their job better, which increases the efficiency of the whole organization. When Ooka Tadasuke became the shogunate administrator for Edo, he was in a position to use his abilities to best advantage, and this was a real blessing for the people of Edo.

A leader must carefully consider the natural abilities of each member of his organization, and must always be careful to match a round peg with a round hole.

In addition, a leader must constantly ask whether he himself is the right man for the job, or whether there is not someone else more suitable. A foot soldier in the wrong job will not do much harm, but if a general is in the wrong job, it may spell defeat for the whole army. A leader must always be sure that he and his subordinates are the right people for the position they occupy.

66

Study Your Rivals

A leader should
learn from his adversaries

TOKUGAWA IEYASU RARELY LOST a battle. Even Toyotomi Hideyoshi suffered an overwhelming defeat at his hands. But Ieyasu finally met his match in Takeda Shingen. Although Ieyasu's army was by far the stronger, Shingen was simply a superior military commander. All of Ieyasu's efforts were to no avail and his army suffered a terrible defeat, with Ieyasu himself only just surviving.

Shortly afterward, Shingen died in action. When he heard the news, Ieyasu paid the following tribute to his rival.

"A truly great man has died. Takeda Shingen was one of the greatest generals of all time, and since my youth I have learned a great deal about tactics simply by observing him. You could almost call him my tutor.

Besides, it did my domain good to have a strong enemy nearby: it spurred my government and army on to greater efforts. Without such an adversary, we would have become lax through inaction and complacency. Shingen was my enemy, to be sure, but his death is a source of genuine grief to me, and no cause for rejoicing."

* * *

Nowadays, the average businessman would regard it as most unfortunate to find his company pitted against a really strong and well-managed competitor. But by adopting Ieyasu's attitude, he could learn a great deal about management from his rival. Even though it is hard to compete against such a strong adversary, it is also a very good incentive to do better, and, in the final analysis, helpful to the development of his own company. If you can accept this outlook, you will be flexible enough to learn from your adversary's strengths, and develop your own potential. Eventually, you may attain the wisdom you need to overcome your rival.

Ieyasu's greatness was no doubt largely a matter of temperament, but I think his willingness to learn from his enemy was also a contributory factor.

67

Common Property

**A leader should
regard his position
as one of public trust**

TOYOTOMI HIDEYOSHI'S ARMY HAD surrounded Akechi
Mitsuharu in Sakamoto Castle. Mitsuharu could not
bear to allow the destruction of the countless rare and
valuable objects within, so when the end seemed immi-
nent, he lowered a message to the enemy commander,
one of Hideyoshi's generals. The message read:

"Objects of great importance are only the temporary
possessions of their owner while he is alive. They are
not private property, but public possessions and the
treasures of the world. My brief private tenure of these
objects is now at an end, but I pray that they will have a
long life as public treasures. To consign them to the
flames would be a great loss to the country, and I would
be sorry if future generations were to see me as a
heartless warrior, responsible for such destruction.

Therefore, I charge you with their safekeeping."

When Toyotomi Hideyoshi heard of this action, he was very impressed. "On the day his castle on Mount Shiki was destroyed, Matsunaga Hisahide smashed a precious tea urn because he could not bear anyone else to have it. What a world of difference between his attitude and Akechi Mitsuharu's. Such a cool-headed and praiseworthy samurai!"

* * *

Nowadays, much is privately owned. Just about everything belongs to one person or another, and these rights of ownership are enshrined in the law. Superficially, individuals possess things, but I believe that on a higher plane, all material things are, as Mitsuharu said, "public possessions and the treasures of the world."

In the running of a business, for example, a certain amount of capital is collected, a plot of land is occupied, resources are used, and people are employed. According to the law, these things may be the possessions of individuals, or of the company. But neither the capital, nor the land, nor the resources, nor the staff, are essentially private possessions: they belong to the world. We are only allowed to label them private possessions for the sake of convenience, so that we can make best use of them for the benefit of society. This truth is not confined to the world of business, it applies everywhere.

A leader must be fully aware that, in essence, everything belongs to the people, everything is public property. As a leader, it, therefore, follows that everything you do is essentially public business. It is important to realize this.

68

When It Rains,
Use an Umbrella

A good leader is guided
by the laws of nature

ONE OF THE MOST profound pieces of wisdom in the Chinese classic the *Laozi* is the following: "If a ruler keeps to the path, matters will take care of themselves." Here the path is not the path of moral virtue, but the broader concept of heaven's dispensation, or the laws of nature. In essence, if a leader follows the laws of nature, affairs of state will proceed smoothly.

* * *

I believe this to be perfectly true. Throughout the cosmos, great laws of nature are at work, and all creatures obey them in one way or another. Human beings are no exception: the only difference between us and other living creatures is that we are blessed with greater understanding, which has enabled us to live in an enlightened and civilized state.

On a superficial level, enlightenment and civilization appear to be man's creation, but in fact this is not so. We have done no more than discover and use what already existed, created by nature. In other words, what we have achieved has been the result of following the laws of nature and using them in our shared human existence.

Human beings, however, tend to forget this and assume that enlightenment and civilization are all their own work. Man is often carried away by his puny human cleverness, and adopts attitudes that go against the laws of nature. Herein lies the ultimate source of all human misery and conflict. For this very reason, it is extremely important that a leader be familiar with these rules and abide by them.

In simple terms, to obey the laws of nature is to do the obvious. When it rains, for example, you put up your umbrella to stop yourself getting wet. This is only common sense. If you take care to do the commonsensical thing at all times, you will make fewer mistakes and you will be well on the way to achieving success and growth.

To run a good business, you must develop a good product, sell it at a reasonable price—though high enough to guarantee a fair profit—and collect payments punctually. In theory, this is not particularly difficult.

In practice, however, it is not at all easy. People get carried away by their own desires and feelings, and forget to apply common sense. For this very reason, a leader must take good care to follow the laws of nature.

69

A Sense of Destiny

*A leader must realize
that his role is only partially
determined by his will*

CONFUCIUS, IN HIS TRAVELS, visited many kingdoms. When he came to a place called Kuang, he was mistaken for someone else, arrested, and imprisoned. His disciples were greatly worried, but he reassured them, saying, "I am trying to spread the word of the ancient sages. This is my destiny. Heaven has sent me on this mission, and as long as heaven does not destroy me, the people of Kuang can do me no harm. Do not worry."

*   *   *

It is very difficult to say whether there is such a thing as fate or destiny. Since the existence of fate cannot be proved scientifically, many argue that fate does not exist. Confucius, however, believed in fate, and at the age of fifty declared that he knew the will of heaven.

Confucius studied the path of virtue practiced by the sages of old, and lived according to its precepts. He made it his life's work to pass on these teachings to posterity. He believed that he was doing this work not on his own initiative, but at the behest of a greater power, namely destiny. This, I believe, was the source of his extraordinary strength.

If you do something on your own initiative, even if your idea is a good one, circumstances will tend to distract you from your purpose. But try looking at it this way: you do your job partly by your own free will, but you are also being guided by the hand of fate. The realization that you are, in a sense, following your destiny, will produce a sense of relief, and give you the courage not to be agitated by trifles.

If you give the matter any thought, you will agree that it was not your idea to be born a human being, or any particular nationality. This, if you like, was a matter of fate. In this sense, even though you have a certain amount of responsibility as a leader for the way things turn out, and a certain amount of control, it is also true that the forces of destiny are at work. Such forces may not be amenable to logical analysis, but all the same, a leader must have a healthy respect for them.

70

An Alternative to Force

A leader must cultivate virtue if he is to be strong

WHEN WORLD WAR II ended, Chiang Kai-shek (Jian Jieshi) proclaimed that China would "return good for evil," and refrained from demanding reparations from Japan or seeking revenge for the suffering it had caused.

* * *

The saying "return good for evil" is attributed to *Laozi*. This principle was transmuted into a tradition which influenced the thinking of leaders in China for two and a half millennia. It is said, for example, that when Zhuge Liang compelled the savage border tribes to submit, he did not simply crush them by force of arms, but captured and released them seven times until he finally won their agreement.

It is quite easy to make people do something. They can be coerced by force, or authority, or reason. When told, "Do this or you will be killed," most people value their lives sufficiently to do as they are told, albeit unwillingly. If people are forced to do something against their will, however, the result will never be wholly satisfactory. The best method is to cultivate virtue, and thereby win people's hearts.

Buddha is said to have possessed such great virtue that even a huge and fearsome elephant knelt at his feet. Even if you yourself do not achieve these heights as a leader, you must be virtuous enough to win the affection of those under your command before you can exert your full authority and apply your other abilities.

As a leader, you must work hard at cultivating virtue. Some people will oppose you and antagonize you. You may use a certain amount of force to counteract such opposition, but this in itself will generally give rise to more resistance. Even when using force, try hard to take account of the other person's feelings, and never forget to look into your own heart. If you cultivate virtue, those who oppose you usually come round to your point of view.

71

Self-Reliance

A leader must foster the spirit of independence in himself and others

---

ANDREW CARNEGIE, ALIAS THE "Steel King," was once asked the secret of his success. "The first thing is to be born into a poor family," he said. "When you dive into the troubled waters of life, you must have the determination to swim by yourself. You have to get along without a life buoy, or a life belt, or a single scrap of food. Otherwise, you will never be independent. An independent spirit is vital. In this sense, the child of a poor family, who starts out with nothing, has a huge advantage over the child of rich parents."

* * *

This is something Carnegie learned from bitter experience. He was the child of a poor immigrant family who worked hard from boyhood onward to better himself, and eventually became a millionaire.

Whatever you do in life, you will never achieve true success if you lack a self-reliant spirit and instead look to others for help. When a person or a company relies too much on someone else's money and skills, and lacks independence, he cannot hope to make progress. In the same way, if a nation relies for its existence on the money, resources, or capital of other countries, then it will be fundamentally weak.

During the oil crises of the 1970s, the Japanese nation was thrown into confusion. The country had lost its independent outlook, and had become too reliant on others. By contrast, under Mao Zedong, neighboring China stuck to a national policy of self-reliance and self-regeneration and made steady progress.

A leader's first priority should be to cultivate a spirit of self-reliance, and maintain it steadfastly. At the same time, those under his command should also be given the chance to learn to be self-reliance. However independent the leader is, it will not do for his subordinates to be overly reliant on him.

Fukuzawa Yukichi, a leading figure of the Meiji period, once said, "Those who lack the spirit of independence give scant thought to their country."

If tens of thousands of people gather together, yet lack the spirit of independence, they are no better than a flock of sheep. If employees of a company lack a spirit of independence, their company will stagnate.

As a leader, you must realize that to cultivate self-reliance is the only way to keep your company, your organization, or your nation on a steady course of growth and strong enough to adapt to changing circumstances.

72

Keep an Open Mind

**A leader should
never shackle himself
to any single idea**

AT THE END OF the Tokugawa period in the nineteenth century, even the samurai warriors who formed the military ruling class had lost their taste for battle. The Choshu domain, for example, although it adopted the slogan "expel the barbarians," made a poor showing when it actually faced off against a foreign power. The weakness and uselessness of the samurai were openly criticized by the farmers and merchants.

It was about this time that Takasugi Shinsaku organized a militia known as the *kiheitai*. Soldiers were recruited on the basis of their willingness and ability to fight, irrespective of their social status. As a result, not only lower-ranking samurai but also farmers, merchants, and hunters flocked to join up. Takasugi imposed strict discipline, and the soldiers were subjected to rigorous training. As a result, when they met in battle, the kiheitai thoroughly routed the all-samurai Choshu army and made outstanding military gains.

* * *

Although the samurai had been weakened by long years of peace, the prevailing view at that time was that war was essentially samurai business. The idea of an army being recruited from the general populace and of conscripts being treated on an equal footing as professional soldiers was received with much hostility. These were uncertain times, and new ideas were accepted with reluctance.

But Takasugi Shinsaku took this bold step because he had sized up the situation. He saw that the power and influence of the samurai were on the wane, and that he had to gather about him men of wider capabilities.

Given human nature, once a certain idea has taken hold, its influence is very strong. It is particularly hard to break free from old ideas and entrenched opinions. Nevertheless, times change: what was taken for granted yesterday may not hold true today.

As a leader, you should be circumspect about old ideas and set notions, and always try to see things with fresh eyes. If you can, you will be able to achieve progress and growth.

73

Work at It

---

*A good leader
recognizes that all-out effort is
the key to success*

THOMAS EDISON, THE KING of inventors, once made the
following reply to someone who praised his genius:
"Genius is 1 percent inspiration and 99 percent perspiration."

No one would hesitate to call Edison a genius. He
was, after all, the man responsible for the incandescent
light bulb, the gramophone, moving pictures, as well as
many other marvelous inventions that could only spring
from the mind of a genius. But Edison himself claimed
that his achievements were not the result of innate
ability but the product of perspiration, or in other
words, effort.

Innumerable anecdotes about Edison illustrate how
hard he worked and studied. Once he started an experiment, he would become so absorbed that he would

literally forget to eat or sleep, oblivious to the passage of time. When someone asked him what the secret of success was, he is said to have replied, "Don't look at your watch." It is even said that he invented the electric lamp largely because it annoyed him that the darkness interfered with his experiments. Edison, who was thought to be backward as a child and withdrawn from junior school, became the king of inventors through tireless effort.

* * *

You and I bemoan our lack of ability and tend to use this as an excuse for unfinished projects. To be sure, native talent is very important in some respects. In sumo wrestling, for example, those who attain the rank of champion have probably been blessed with the right physical attributes. Nevertheless, the sad truth is that many wrestlers who have the right disposition and are expected to become future champions end up not making the grade. The most common reason for this is insufficient training—in other words, not enough effort.

Before you complain about your temperament or your ability, first ask yourself how much effort you have put in. Everyone should do this, especially a leader. As Edison said, the idea—the inspiration—is vital; without it, nothing would ever be produced. But no matter how good the idea, you will achieve nothing if you just sit back and wait for things to happen: bringing the idea to life takes sustained, all-out effort. Edison's unstinting effort is a great lesson to leaders in all fields.

74

Look to the Long-Term

A leader shouldn't be
blinded by short-term prospects

TOYOTOMI HIDEYOSHI HAD THE Mori family surrounded. But when he received news that Oda Nobunaga had been treacherously killed by Akechi Mitsuhide, he made a treaty with them and turned back. Although many of his associates were strongly in favor of breaking the treaty and pursuing Hideyoshi, but the Mori family's vice commander, Kobayakawa Takakage, argued against this. "War has lasted 100 years, but is now drawing to a close," he said. "This is Hideyoshi's hour, and after Nobunaga's demise, power will naturally fall to him. If we break this treaty and earn Hideyoshi's enmity, the house of Mori will be doomed. We would do better to keep faith with this treaty, and share in Hideyoshi's future ascendancy."

The family was won over by this speech, and decided

to pursue the policy of reconciliation. Sure enough, Hideyoshi later destroyed Mitsuhide and rose to power. He was very appreciative of those who had shown him loyalty, and richly rewarded the Mori family and Takakage.

*   *   *

People tend to be preoccupied with the short-term, and thereby lose sight of the long-term issues. Of course, we are continually faced with problems requiring immediate action, and it is very important to take appropriate action in these cases. If we are to do the right thing and avoid mistakes, however, it is vital to bear in mind the long-term issues when we decide how to deal with short-term ones.

A decision which results in a temporary advantage will often lead to a greater loss in the long run, and, conversely, something which appears to be a loss in the short-term will, in the future, turn into a solid gain. This would seem to be obvious, but all too often people tend to base decisions on the immediate prospects. Kobayakawa Takakage was concerned with the long-term stability of the house of Mori, and his foresight paid off.

75

Staying on Course

A leader must do
what has to be done

FUKUZAWA YUKICHI, ONE OF the leading lights of the Meiji era, used to teach economics using English-language textbooks at his school in Tokyo, which later came to be known as Keio University. During the turbulent Meiji Restoration, classes went on as usual even when the sounds of a nearby battle encroached.

Fukuzawa encouraged his students with these words: "When Holland was occupied during the Napoleonic wars, the Dutch compound on Dejima Island in Nagasaki was the only place in the world where the Dutch flag still flew. On the strength of this one free Dutch community, the Dutch boasted that their country had never been totally conquered. In the same way, the thread of Western learning in Japan remains unbroken, no matter how much disturbance and upheaval is going on around us. As long as this school exists, Japan is one of the world's enlightened countries. Do not concern yourselves now with the outside world."

*　*　*

"Clothe thee in war, arm thee in peace," goes the saying. Even during peacetime, we must not neglect to prepare our heart and mind for upheaval. But the saying, "Forget not peace in time of war," is equally as important, reminding us that even in the midst of chaos we must remain calm and detached about what needs to be done.

Fukuzawa Yukichi traveled abroad on his own account, and took note of the direction in which the world was heading. He became deeply absorbed in Western learning, and saw it as his duty to give a practical education to the bright young men who one day would put Japan back on its feet. Even when a battle in the vicinity of his school seemed increasingly likely, he continued to study Western learning, and threw himself into educating the young.

We all of us tend to be swept along by the prevailing circumstances. In peacetime, we give never a thought to war, and in time of war, we can see no further than the upheaval around us. If we are to remain detached, and confidently follow an independent path, it is vital to consider what must be done, and then do it wholeheartedly. A firm grasp of this point is important for any individual, and of course imperative for a leader.

Whatever the circumstances, remain detached from them. If you keep a cool head and get the job done, everyone will follow you. I would even go so far as to say that the secret of leadership is as simple as doing what has to be done.

76

Put People First

A leader must be humane in his dealings with others

WHEN TOYOTOMI HIDEYOSHI'S ADOPTED daughter fell ill and it was widely thought she was possessed by a fox spirit, Hideyoshi reportedly sent the following official letter, stamped with his seal, to Inari Daimyojin, the fox spirit shrine. "It is inexcusable of you," he wrote, "to possess a human being in this way, but I am willing to forgive this one occasion. If, however, you ever repeat this offense, I shall order the whole of Japan to hold an annual fox hunt. All persons and creatures in this country are under my charge. Therefore, be gone from her at once!"

*   *   *

It was not unusual for a statesman to send official

documents stamped with their seals to Shinto priests, but Hideyoshi is apparently the only statesman ever to send a command to the fox spirit of Inari Daimyojin. Missives to Buddhist and Shinto deities normally took the form of letters of supplication. Some would have thought Hideyoshi's action extremely impertinent.

Evidently Hideyoshi did not think so. In his view, as chief imperial advisor, he was acting in the emperor's name, and was, therefore, responsible for the security of the Japanese people. If any being, even a divinity, threatened the happiness of the people, it was his duty, as a statesman, to deal with him. One could argue with his approach, but Hideyoshi's reasoning—the fact that he put the people first in such a situation—is extremely interesting.

If we are going to make the world a better place, and increase the sum of human happiness, mankind must know itself. We should understand what it means to be human, and how humans should behave. If we are thoughtless and needlessly cruel, then all our efforts will prove fruitless and result instead in human suffering.

As a leader, you must strive to be humane. Use this as a basis for leading your life and it will prove to be a true source of strength.

77

Empathy

A leader must understand the inner workings of human nature

"WELL FED, WELL BRED" is a remark attributed to Guan Zhong, a statesman who lived in the kingdom of Qi in ancient China. "People only have good manners when their granary is full," he said, "and people only know right from wrong when they have the necessities of life."

Guan Zhong placed great importance on morals. He knew that if the people strayed from the path of virtue, then the country would be ruined. But he also knew that virtue must be backed up by material plenty—in other words, by full granaries and good supplies of life's necessities. To encourage virtue, he devised ways to make the economy thrive and increase the country's wealth. As a result, the small kingdom of Qi became the strongest in the whole of China.

Guan Zhong understood men, and had a sharp insight into the inner workings of the human mind. This is what enabled him to make such pithy remarks and carry out such skillful statecraft. He is said to have made all his government ordinances easy to understand and execute, on the grounds that, "government ordinance should be in tune with popular feelings."

* * *

Human nature is not amenable to logical analysis. While something may be logically the right thing to do, a person will often want to do quite the opposite. Human nature certainly has its troublesome aspects, but it does follow certain patterns and principles. An ability to understand these patterns and principles is what I mean by a knowledge of the inner workings of the human mind.

If you lack this knowledge, and try to work by logic or reason alone, you will come up against opposition, experience problems, and end up with little reward for your pains. If you persist, and try to force people to do things your way, you may end up by hurting people. Consider the achievements of outstanding statesmen and leaders in history, and you will see that all of them had a good grasp of the subtleties of human nature, and applied their knowledge to the task at hand.

The best way to learn the finer points of human nature is to mix with a wide range of people in a wide variety of situations. Anyone who wants to be a leader should have as much experience as possible of the world. A leader must always bear this experience in mind so that he can look at people objectively and divine their orientation.

78

All Fired Up

A leader must be
enthusiastic to be effective

DURING CHINA'S WARRING STATES period, there lived a
man called Su Qin. Although just a commoner, he
wanted to give the country's rulers the benefit of his
learning, so he went from kingdom to kingdom, dis-
pensing wisdom. At first, no one would listen to him,
but eventually he was received by the king of Yan.
China then consisted of seven kingdoms: Yan, Qin,
Zhao, Qi, Wei, Han, and Chu. The western kingdom
of Qin was gradually gaining ascendancy and oppres-
sing the other kingdoms. Su Qin, having found a foot-
hold in Yan, visited Cho, Han, Wei, Qi, and Chu in
turn, and urged each ruler to join in opposing Qin. Each
of the kings was moved by his argument, and eventually Su Qin became the joint prime minister of all
six kingdoms. The isolated kingdom of Qin was un-

able to attack the others for the next fifteen years.

*   *   *

During this period in China's history, rulers would often seek out men of talent in other kingdoms, and it was not unusual for such men to rise to important positions by virtue of their strong will and powers of persuasion. Nevertheless, Su Qin, who became prime minister of six kingdoms and held sway over the whole of China, stood out even in this distinguished company.

His success was no doubt partly due to effective tactics and eloquent speech, but I believe that his keen determination also played a part. For example, it took him over a year to obtain his first audience with the king of Yan, long after a normal man would have given up. Subsequently, he brought the whole of China round to his way of thinking—an enormous undertaking. Being able to maintain his enthusiasm for the task at hand was the secret of his success.

Enthusiasm is half the battle in pursuing any matter. If you are half-hearted, you will never get anywhere. Only when you have the enthusiasm to see your cause through at all costs will you discover the wisdom and the resources to succeed.

As leader, you must be more enthusiastic than anyone else. Others may outdo you in terms of intelligence or talent, but you must be second to none when it comes to enthusiasm. If you are enthusiastic enough to persevere whatever happens, this is bound to rub off on your followers. Moved by your enthusiasm, the intelligent people will contribute their ideas and insights, and the talented people their special gifts. A leader need never worry because he lacks a particular talent; what he should worry about is lack of enthusiasm.

79

The Aura of Authority

A leader must cultivate charisma

DATE MASAMUNE HESITATED WHEN Toyotomi Hideyoshi invited him to join forces. But when he saw the superiority of Hideyoshi's army, he had second thoughts, and eventually made his way to Hideyoshi's camp, although he expected to be upbraided for dragging his feet.

Hideyoshi did indeed question him about the delay, but then offered to show him the barracks. He asked Masamune to carry his sword, although he himself was accompanied only by a single page for protection and seemed completely unconcerned by his apparent vulnerability.

When later he was to describe the experience, Date Masamune said, "At that point, fear alone kept me from even thinking of harming Hideyoshi. He was more than a great man, he was a god-like figure."

Masamune was completely enthralled. Nor was he the only one: many of Hideyoshi's other enemies were later won over to his side.

* * *

Hideyoshi evidently had a great deal of personal magnetism. This may have been innate, or the result of skillful application of the comprehensive knowledge of human nature that he acquired as a youth, when he traveled throughout the country. Whatever the source of Hideyoshi's charisma, men were drawn to him like iron filings to a magnet.

Charisma is a very desirable quality in a leader. If a leader has the magnetism that makes people willing to do anything for him, they will flock about him spontaneously, and work enthusiastically. A man who lacks this quality will never make a really great leader.

Since a person's character is to some extent inherent, not everyone may be able to acquire charisma. But a good knowledge of human nature and consideration of others can add up to a type of charm—given sustained effort. It is also possible to develop attractiveness not just as an individual but through one's company or organization.

At any rate, a leader should realize the importance of charisma and should make every effort to cultivate this quality.

80

Balancing Act

A good leader pays attention to the chemistry of human relations

---

TAKEDA SHINGEN NEVER BUILT a castle in his entire life. Instead, he set great store by his men, and ensured his own position by using their talents to the full. In his own words, "People are the stone walls, people are the castle." He described his ideology as follows.

"I always aim for balance. Baba Nobufusa, for example, is a man of few words and rather conceited. Therefore, I paired him up with a fellow who talks too much but is a brisk worker. Yamagata Masakage is a hothead, and will strike out at an enemy as soon as look at him, with whatever forces he has at the time. Therefore, I put him to work with a man who thinks carefully before he acts, such as Kosaka Masanobu. If you put an obstinate man together with a meek man and define their roles, then like fire and water, they will bring things to the boil between them."

* * *

A properly balanced team is very important for getting the most out of people. In matching an employee to the position it is important to ensure he has the right workmates.

Each employee has his strong points and his weak points. Put people in teams which allow them to compensate for one another's weak points, and they will all be able to give of their best. Then again, there is the subtle question of compatibility—not an easy matter to quantify. If a personality clash occurs, the parties involved should try to minimize any discord, but it is also important to arrange work teams so that such problems do not occur in the first place.

Illustrations of the compatibility problem are not hard to find. How many times have I seen examples of, say, three people being assigned to work together, and although each one is an excellent worker, for some reason the work does not go well. Their boss then steps in and transfers one of the three to another project, leaving the other two to do the job. In a very short space of time, their productivity more than doubles, and the other person also achieves a great deal more in his new position.

It does not necessarily follow that a team of outstanding, highly intelligent people will produce the best results. Conversely, less outstanding workers can achieve great things if they are assigned to a well-balanced team. A leader must be a consummate master of the art of matching up people.

81

Strict Regimens

**A leader must
apply rigorous standards
when training subordinates**

NEAR KOISHIKAWA IN EDO, the territory of the Mito
domain, there was an execution ground known as Saku-
ra no Baba. One evening young Tokugawa Mitsukuni
was ordered by his father, Yorifusa, to go and fetch the
head of a criminal who had been executed that morning. The execution ground—a thickly wooded spot for-
bidding even in the daytime—was held in dread by clan
retainers, but Mitsukuni showed no fear and set off to
do as he was bid. He groped about until he found the
head, but it proved too heavy and awkward for him to
carry, so he returned home, dragging it along after him.
Seeing the struggling figure of his son, Yorifusa felt
great joy and satisfaction at the boy's courage.

* * *

Yorifusa's command was a test of courage. To us, it seems extremely cruel to send a child to fetch the head of a corpse, but it was using this type of rigorous discipline that the lords of those times trained their sons.

People develop through training. A world class athlete's performance looks quite effortless, but is in fact the result of rigorous training. Training can be carried out on the spiritual level as well as the physical or technical level. The ascetic practices of Zen Buddhism, for example, are extremely strict. A normal person would find them unbearable, but a monk who has undergone ascetic training can follow them without suffering any hardship.

With strict training, people can achieve limitless mental and physical heights. Conversely, without training, they will never fulfill their potential, no matter how outstanding their innate gifts.

To bring out the best in people, you must invest a great deal of effort in training them. Of course, many of the methods used in the past are hardly applicable today, and would even be counterproductive. Nevertheless, some form of rigorous schooling must be provided, and the question of training must never be neglected.

82

True Education

A leader should awaken his people to their worth as human being

---

WHEN YOSHIDA SHOIN WAS twenty-three years old, he attempted to stow away aboard Commodore Matthew Perry's flagship. Discovered, he was arrested and thrown in jail. There were eleven other prisoners at the time, and Shoin was soon on friendly terms with them. The prison became a classroom where the prisoners educated one another: Shoin gave lectures on the Nine Chinese Classics, while a prisoner skilled in haiku gave classes on poetry; another inmate, who was an excellent calligrapher, taught this skill to the rest. The prison had hitherto been a place of despair, but through this mutual education, the men regained their confidence and courage, and the whole atmosphere changed. This came to the notice of the domain authorities, who eventually released them all.

*   *   *

Most people would find it impossible to keep their spirits up in jail. Yoshida Shoin not only managed to do this, but also educated the other prisoners at the same time. Moreover, this was education in its true sense: by teaching them and learning from them, he made them forget their prison walls, and opened their eyes to their value and dignity as human beings.

Upon his release, Shoin established his famous private academy, the Shoka Sonjuku, and it is surely no accident that among its alumni were those who later played key roles in overthrowing the shogunate and returning power to the emperor in the Meiji Restoration. Pupils included not only the sons of high-ranking families but also those of lower-order samurai, such as Ito Hirobumi and Yamagata Aritomo. In feudal times, the latter would not normally have attained important positions, yet they eventually became pillars of the Japanese nation. Of course, their own outstanding natural talents helped them reach the top, but it was the educational opportunity provided by Yoshida Shoin that helped draw out their hidden qualities.

While incarcerated, Yoshida Shoin composed these lines: "The Japanese spirit which, even while knowing fully the consequences, cannot help but act nonetheless." He would not have felt such sincere concern for the future of his country unless his eyes had been opened to the value of all human beings, including prisoners and commoners.

In educating people, the most important thing you can teach is not facts, not knowledge, but human dignity. This will awaken them.

83

The Key to Greatness

---

*A leader must know
how to use people with abilities
surpassing his own*

LIU BANG, FOUNDER OF the Han empire, once had the following conversation with his subordinate, the famous commander Han Xin.

"How many soldiers could I command?"
"Your majesty could command 100,000 men at most."
"And you?"
"I could command many more."
"Then why are you my subordinate?"
"Because your majesty is not a commander of soldiers, but a commander of commanders."

Han Xin, who led the army to victory, was far superior in terms of military skill, but the emperor had the ability to use his commander in the right way. As the emperor himself said to Han Xin, "I cannot plan a campaign half as well as can my general, Zhang Liang. In administrative skill, my minister Xu He is by far my superior. When it comes to leading an army to certain victory, I am no match for you, commander. Each one of you is a genius in his own field. But I know how best to utilize your talents. That is why I am emperor."

* * *

This is an interesting point. Compared with each of the three men, the emperor's abilities were not outstanding: there were probably any number of men much more accomplished than he. But Liu Bang, who had risen from humble beginnings to unite the vast nation of China, and who laid the foundations for an empire that endured for hundreds of years, had the key to greatness: he knew how to use subordinates whose abilities were greater than his own.

Liu Bang's sovereignty was constantly challenged by Xiang Yu, a remarkable warrior renowned for his strength and wisdom. But, as Liu Bang pointed out, "Xiang Yu could not even make proper use of his own general, Fan Zeng!"

However capable a man may be, he can only do so much on his own. A man who is unable to handle people will never make an outstanding leader. It is only when we learn to use our subordinates and listen to what they say, that we take our first step toward greatness. Able people tend to put too much faith in their own abilities, and often fail to make the best use of their subordinates. This is something every leader should bear in mind.

84

Tailor Your Approach

A leader must be able to present the same issue in different ways to different people

---

ONE OF THE EVENTS described in the Romance of the Three Kingdoms is the famous battle of Chi Bi. Cao Cao of Wei threatened Sun Quan of Wu with an army of 1 million men, and the kingdom of Wu was divided over the question of whether to fight or sue for peace. In neighboring Shu, one of King Liu Bei's retainers, Zhuge Liang, realized that if Wu sued for peace, it would fall into the hands of Cao Cao. He, therefore, journeyed to Wu in order to persuade Sun Quan to stand his ground.

A Wu hawk advised Zhuge Liang to encourage Sun Quan to fight by playing down Wei's military strength. But when Zhuge Liang was questioned by Sun Quan about the Wei army, he replied, "They are said to number a million, but actually there are even more of them, and they are all hand-picked. It would be wise to seek peace at this point." Surprised, Sun Quan asked, "Then why does Liu Bei want to fight Cao Cao if his army is even weaker than ours?"

Zhuge Liang replied, "My lord is fighting the traitor Cao Cao so that he can restore the Han empire. He will fight for honor, so the question of victory or defeat is secondary. But if Wu's chief priority is its own security, I would advise a peace treaty." This struck a chord in Sun Quan's heart, and he resolved to fight Cao Cao. Sun Quan's army joined forces with Liu Bei's to win a great victory which left its mark on history.

*   *   *

Zhuge Liang knew that Sun Quan was a great warrior, and unlikely to be easily manipulated by petty tricks such as pretending that the Wei army was smaller than it actually was. Instead, he took a bold approach, with great success — a perfect example of a leader tailoring his approach to suit the individual.

No matter how good your ideas, they are of little value unless they are acted upon by other people. Nor can you assume that just because your plans are good they will be accepted. People need to be persuaded. Good persuasive technique consists largely of tailoring your approach to suit the person you are trying to persuade. The important thing is to use the right approach for the individual with whom you are dealing, appealing to his sense of honor, desire for profit, emotions, or his reason.

Before you can do this, you need a certain amount of knowledge and experience. Thus, a leader must continually try out new techniques of persuasion and must always try to learn more about human nature.

85

Putting Together a Team

A leader should surround himself with the right people

LIU BEI, KING OF Shu, was a descendant of the imperial Han family. As a young man, he was forced to weave and sell straw mats to make a living because of his family's poverty. Despite this, he was determined to restore the Han dynasty to its proper place, a goal he eventually achieved. Contributing to his success was his penchant for picking capable people, in particular Zhuge Liang, the driving force behind Liu Bei's rise.

Even as a young man, Zhuge Liang's talents were highly regarded. But although he was ambitious, he did not approach Liu Bei and chose instead to live in the countryside, keeping to himself. Liu Bei visited Zhuge's thatched cottage three times to pay his respects and urge him to become a retainer. Liu Bei's enthusiasm and sincerity impressed Zhuge Liang and eventually he agreed to serve the monarch. Rejoiced Liu, "Now that I have Zhuge Liang with me, I am like a fish that has found water!"

Liu treated Zhuge Liang so well that at first the leading Shu warriors were jealous. They eventually recognized that Zhuge Liang's outstanding tactical skills were helping them to win victories, which made it easier for them to accept his exalted position. Once he had Zhuge working for him, Liu Bei was able to make rapid progress.

* * *

Surrounding yourself with the right people is vital if you want to get things done. As Liu himself was to note, "People can build up a kingdom, and people can bring it down." The basis of business is people and the very success or failure of any project ultimately depends finally on the people carrying it out.

How does a leader gather the right people? Generally speaking, although luck and destiny play a part, people gravitate toward you when you start to look for them, but good people will not materialize around you unasked. The gods help those who help themselves: only when a leader actively searches for good people will they come to him.

Liu Bei was prepared to look hard for what he wanted. Against the advice of his other retainers, he visited Zhuge Liang three times to ask him to join him. Liu's genuine desire to find good people made a strong impression on Zhuge Liang, and also drew many other brave generals and wise retainers to him.

The world seems to be full of leaders who complain about a shortage of good personnel. I ask them to ask themselves just how hard they have really searched.

86

Every Day Is a New Beginning

A leader must take a fresh look at the world daily

KING TANG, THE LEGENDARY founder of the Yin dynasty in ancient China, was said to have been a benevolent and wise ruler. Even Confucius praised his virtue and wisdom, describing him as a model for other leaders to follow. Engraved on the inside of King Tang's washbasin were the words: "If you start the day afresh, and do so everyday, each day will be a new beginning."

If you make a genuine effort to start every day afresh, you will gradually learn to look at the world anew every day. King Tang had this personal motto inscribed on his washbasin so that it was the first thing he saw daily.

* * *

King Tang was said to have lived about 3,000 years ago. In those days, the pace of change was very slow and the passing of ten years probably seemed, as the saying goes, "like a single day." So if King Tang saw the necessity to make a fresh start every day, even those slow-moving times, he must truly have been a great leader.

These days, change happens all the time. What you hold as a basic truth today may be outdated tomorrow. Consequently, you will never be successful if you stick to rigid patterns of thought and let ten years pass as though they were a single day.

As a leader, you must be quick to spot the subtlest changes in the world, constantly updating your leadership philosophy and revising your strategies accordingly. It is vital to avoid getting stuck in a rut. Avoid this by taking a fresh look at the world every day.

Let us move a little further forward in history. Buddha, who lived about 2,500 years ago, preached that all phenomena are transitory in nature. Around the same time, the Greek philosopher Heraclitus taught that everything changes and that even the sun we see today is different from the sun we saw yesterday.

Since ancient times, messiahs and sages everywhere have stressed the need to make a fresh start daily. In this age of rapid progress, it is more important than ever for a leader not to get stuck in a rut.

87

Look Around You

A leader must maintain a broad perspective

WHEN STILL A YOUNG man, Saigo Takamori told Shimazu Nariakira, his liege, "My lord, people are saying that you have come under the influence of the West."

"This is a time of national emergency," Nariakira replied. "Japan is exhausted, and the foreign powers are just waiting for an opening. Western civilization is highly advanced, and Japan's strength is no match. I believe we must turn our eyes to the outside world, emulating the strong points of Western culture and strengthening our weaknesses. In this way, we can make Japan one of the world's leading nations.

"Do not forget that Japanese culture has already borrowed many things from China that we have made our own. The criticism of narrow-minded people who know nothing of the outside world does not bother me.

You, too, must broaden your horizons."

* * *

Although Nariakira did not altogether succeed in his objectives, he is still regarded by many people as the most important daimyo of the last days of the Tokugawa shogunate. Katsu Kaishu gave him the highest accolade when he wrote, "It was Shimazu Nariakira who paved the way for the opening of Japan." Shimazu's follower, Saigo Takamori, was very active in the Meiji Restoration and it is said that his outstanding career owed much to the training he received from his lord.

Nariakira is now seen as a wise ruler because he looked beyond the affairs of his clan. He took account of the world situation, how this would affect Japan's future, and the role his domain should play. From this perspective, he was able to make proposals both to the imperial court and the ruling warrior class, influence other great men, train his samurai, and generally pave the way for Japan's opening.

Breadth of vision is an indispensable quality in a leader. If you look no further than the boundaries of your own country, company, or group, you will be more likely to make mistakes. Things have changed a great deal since the last days of the Tokugawa shogunate and the Meiji Restoration. Today, news of an event occurring in one corner of the globe is transmitted nearly instantaneously all over the world.

A leader must look at the big picture. Whatever your business, you need to know about the outside world because it affects you and your organization. You should also point out the importance of breadth of vision to those you lead.

88

Nothing Is Impossible

A leader can achieve anything if he doesn't flout the laws of nature

---

EVERYONE KNOWS NAPOLEON'S FAMOUS dictum: "The word 'impossible' is not in my dictionary." This may seem a rather dubious claim as Napoleon himself found it impossible to succeed in his campaign to rule Europe. He was eventually defeated by a grand alliance of European powers, taken captive, and exiled to a lonely island where he ended his days.

* * *

Mere vainglory? Perhaps. But looked at from a different perspective, Napoleon's phrase contains a grain of truth. To be sure, we cannot do things that go against the laws of nature. Take immortality, for example. Since the laws of nature dictate that everyone will die sooner or later, we cannot live forever, however much we might want to.

But the converse of this is that anything that doesn't go against the laws of nature is possible. If an enterprise is run in accordance with the laws of nature, I believe it is bound to succeed. The way to this success is simple: make a good product, sell it at a reasonable price, and collect all the money owed. Do this consistently, and you will be 100 percent successful. If you are not successful, it will be because you have run counter to the laws of nature in some way, either by producing a poor product, setting your price too high, or failing to collect the money owed you.

In the *Sun-tzu* is written: "He who knows his enemy and himself will never lose, no matter how many battles he fights." To know your enemy and to know yourself is to fight a battle in accordance with the laws of nature.

Looked at in this light, Napoleon's dictum has some validity. As long as you obey the laws of nature, are determined, and do what has to be done, there is nothing a human being cannot achieve. Anything which you consider impossible is impossible only because you believe it to be so.

Napoleon claimed that nothing was impossible, but he met with defeat. As a leader, ask yourself why Napoleon failed, and take the lesson to heart.

89

Give a Clear Lead

A leader should take firm decisions and make sure his followers understand them

---

AKECHI MITSUHIDE'S 13,000 SOLDIERS received orders from Oda Nobunaga to attack the house of Mori. They set off under Mitsuhide's command, but en route he told them of a dramatic change of plan. "The real enemy is Oda Nobunaga," he declared, and gave the order to attack. The 13,000 soldiers descended the unsuspecting Nobunaga in Kyoto like an avalanche, and Mitsuhide's treacherous rebellion succeeded perfectly.

*   *   *

Leaving aside the question of why Mitsuhide fell upon his lord in this way and whether or not it was a good decision, there is a lesson here for every leader.

When the great general announced his plans, all his subordinates carried out his orders faithfully. It was probably morally wrong to attack Nobunaga, and many of his men must have had their doubts about being involved in such treason. Nevertheless, 13,000 soldiers followed Mitsuhide's order to the letter. This, of course, was partly due to the daily drilling that he had given them, but the main factor was that the troops trusted their commander implicitly.

It is a fact of life is that people will not always do as you want them to. However, once you make a clear decision to go east, however, hardly anyone will openly oppose you and insist on going west, even though they may disagree wholeheartedly with your decision.

As a leader, it is very important that you decide on the path you are going to take and that you make your decision quite clear to your followers. Do this, and they will all move in the same direction in accordance with your policy. That is why you must carefully judge the rights and wrongs of an issue and ensure that your plan is the correct one.

Even when the decision is morally wrong—like the rebellion in this example—once it has been taken it will be carried out. The saying, "If one horse bolts, all horses bolt," applies equally to human beings. If you make a bad decision and bad plans, your followers can only act within the confines of your unfortunate choices.

90

Generosity of Spirit

A leader must be broad-minded enough to forgive opposition

IN THE SPRING AND Autumn period, when China was parceled out among rival warlords, the man regarded as supreme ruler was Duke Huan of Qi. His ascendancy is said to have owed much to the ability of his councilor, Guan Zhong.

Before the duke came to power, there had been a dispute concerning the succession to the imperial throne. At that time, Guan Zhong opposed Duke Huan and even attempted to assassinate him. When Duke Huan was enthroned, he planned to execute Guan Zhong, but his retainers advised him to make use of him to gain supremacy over the whole country. The duke decided to make him his councilor, and was rewarded with a servant who did a great deal to promote the prosperity and military strength of the country. He effectively made Duke Huan supreme ruler.

* * *

If Duke Huan had been mean-spirited enough to seek revenge against his opponents and ignore the good advice of his retainers, he probably would not have succeeded in ruling China. His tolerance and magnanimity in forgiving Guan Zhong and giving him a major role in government led to the consolidation of his own position.

Toyotomi Hideyoshi made much the same point when he said, "Lord [Oda] Nobunaga was a great man, but he bore a deep grudge against anyone who ever opposed him and exacted harsh revenge. I believe this was the reason behind Akechi Mitsuhide's rebellion. When a man surrenders to me, I treat him as gently as if he had always been my retainer. This is how I was able to restore peace to the country so quickly."

If you bear a grudge against someone who has once opposed you, you will feel obliged to pursue the feud to the bitter end. If you welcome a former enemy who has joined you, however, you will have good reason to forgo useless conflict.

When hiring personnel, it is better not to be unduly influenced by people's past attitude toward you, by personal inclination, or by your own prejudices.

As a leader, you must have the generosity of spirit to rise above petty considerations. You should be able to accept all manner of people, using them to the greatest advantage. If you have this quality, people will gravitate to you and it will be easy to assign them the roles which best suit their abilities.

Of the many qualities a good leader should have, magnanimity is one of the most important.

91

Credit Where Credit Is Due

A leader must never stint on giving praise when it is deserved

---

KATO KIYOMASA'S PRINCIPAL OFFICIAL was a samurai by the name of Iida Kakubei, an outstanding warrior and tactician. After Kiyomasa's death, Kakubei did not seek another master but lived in retirement in Kyoto.

"When I first experienced warfare and won military honors," he is reported to have said, "I saw many of my companions wounded and killed by the enemy. I realized then that war is a terrible thing and resolved to quit the soldier's life. However, as soon as I returned from war, Kato Kiyomasa praised my efforts and even presented me with a sword as a token of his satisfaction, so I decided to stay on after all. Whenever I fought in battle after that, I would always think to myself, 'Never again!' Yet every single time, my lord would give me a tabard or a letter of appreciation—

something greatly envied by my companions—and heap praise on me. All of this so turned my head that I never did leave his service, though I always meant to. Looking back, I see that I was very cleverly handled by my lord."

*   *   *

It is interesting to note that even a brave man like Iida Kakubei was so affected by the horrors of war that after every battle he felt like leaving his lord's service. But because of the praise and rewards he received, he stayed on.

A sincere and warm-hearted man, Kato Kiyomasa is unlikely to have used praise cynically or as a method of manipulation—doubtless he praised Kakubei because of the samurai's outstanding military prowess. But notice that Iida Kakubei said his lord praised him "every single time." I can well imagine Kiyomasa looking into Kakubei's face as he returned from the battlefield, telling him, "You fought magnificently! You are an example for others to follow!" then presenting him with a reward on the spot. No wonder this touched Kakubei's heart and won his lifelong devotion.

Everyone likes to be praised. Nothing makes a person feel so alienated as work that goes unappreciated. Praise gives the recipient pleasure and boosts his confidence. It also motivates him to achieve more next time, and acts as an incentive for development.

When people make mistakes or fail at a task, they need to be scolded in no uncertain terms. One of the secrets of good leadership, however, is to be unstinting with praise and rewards when they are deserved.

92

Delegating Responsibility

A leader must make use of other people's abilities rather than relying solely on his own

---

CONFUCIUS HEAPED EXTRAORDINARY PRAISE on one of his young pupils, Zi Jian, calling him "a splendid man." Zi Jian was made deputy governor of a nearby district and although he did little work and spent most of his time playing the zither, his region ran like clockwork. His predecessor had worked extremely hard from morning to night, but had been unable to make the district run smoothly. Puzzled, he asked Zi Jian how he managed it. Replied Zi Jian, "You had a hard time because you tried to do everything yourself. I use my subordinates, and get them to do everything for me."

* * *

Illustrations of this principle are not hard to find

today. Some business managers run their businesses well with little apparent effort, while others try hard with so little result that one feels sorry for them. In many cases, this is because the former know how to use their subordinates, while the latter do not.

Confucius' praise indicates that Zi Jian was an able man whose abilities included the talent to get other people to do his work. His predecessor, however, placed too much faith in his own ability and ended up doing everything himself.

If, as a leader, you try to do everything yourself, you will soon come up against your own limitations. No matter how many hours you put in, you will never be able to manage adequately. If you delegate half-heartedly by trying to supervise everyone too closely, meddling in all the details and giving instructions, you will be a nuisance to your subordinates and they will lose enthusiasm. In the end, you will get little profit for your pains.

When people are given a degree of responsibility and entrusted with a job, they will generally get the job done. As a leader, your task is to keep a firm grasp on the overall picture and establish a clear plan. Then you should give your subordinates responsibility and authority, and let them get on with the work at hand. Do this, and they will use their abilities to the full for you. As a rule, common sense will triumph and the work will go well.

93

Lateral Thinking

A leader must
maintain a flexible approach
to problem-solving

DURING TOYOTOMI HIDEYOSHI'S REIGN, a severe storm caused the Yodogawa river to burst its banks, threatening serious flooding. Hideyoshi went to the scene himself, spurring on the desperate efforts to contain the river. His retainers frantically stacked sandbags where the banks had been breached, but were unable to stem the flood. The rain fell heavier, the water rose higher, and the retainers began to panic.

Into the midst of this confusion stepped Ishida Mitsunari. Quickly assessing the situation, he had a nearby granary opened and ordered his men to carry out several thousand sacks of rice. They piled these on the embankment, sealing the gaps and stemming the torrent.

Eventually the rain stopped and the water level dropped. Mitsunari then asked the local people to make sturdy sandbags and bring them to the embankment. To encourage them, he promised a reward of one sack of rice for each sandbag. Not surprisingly, people vied with one another to bring as many heavy sandbags as they could, and soon the embankment was stronger than ever. Even Toyotomi Hideyoshi was forced to admire Mitsunari's cunning.

* * *

Ishida Mitsunari's first priority had been to find a way to stem the flood and save lives, regardless of how this was achieved. With no more sandbags immediately available, the situation required another solution — bags of rice. But had Mitsunari allowed the sacks of rice to remain at the river once the crisis had been averted, he might have been accused of profligate waste — in those days, rice was the mostly highly prized commodity. But the second part of the solution — paying people with the bags of rice to repair the river banks — was equally adept. In getting the job done so quickly, he showed not just resourcefulness but a capacity for lateral thinking.

The ability to think laterally is a very important quality in a leader. It is much easier to recognize than to emulate, however.

We tend to restrict our own creativity by thinking along standard lines. Try and avoid this by keeping your mind open and your ideas flexible, which will enable you to see things from a new perspective. A leader should try applying lateral thinking in all sorts of situations, thus cultivating the ability to come up with a creative solution every time.

94

Summoning Up Courage

A leader must be able to spur himself on at all times

YAMANAKA SHIKANOSUKE WAS A famous hero in Japan's civil war period. It is said that he often prayed to the gods to send him suffering and hardship. When asked about this strange request, he replied, "Unless a man experiences many things for himself, he will never understand the human heart or know what a human being can achieve. I want to test my ability to withstand all kinds of adversity."

Shikanosuke is also thought to be the author of the lines which read, "Send me more misfortunes, that I might test my puny strength."

* * *

People pray for a wide variety of reasons, but usually

they seek happiness, health, or wealth. They rarely pray for suffering and hardship. It is hardly surprising that Shikanosuke's prayer seemed strange to those around him. No doubt he was hoping to test his strength and steel himself through hardship, but I think he may also have used prayer as a means to summon up his courage.

Yamanaka Shikanosuke's daimyo, Amako, had been routed by the house of Mori, and it was Shikanosuke's dearest wish to restore his lord's house and exact revenge. Mori's forces were growing in strength, however, while Amako's forces were in tatters. Victory over the enemy did not seem possible and all hope was lost. Under these circumstances, Shikanosuke's spirit might well have broken; in fact, it was the answer to his prayer. The suffering and hardship were what spurred him on. The answer to his prayer was his means of summoning up courage to face each new day.

We tend to think that all great men have an endless reservoir of courage and nerves of steel, but this is not so. Even the great Saigo Takamori eventually despaired and drowned himself rather than go on.

A more contemporary hero, U.S. President John F. Kennedy, is known to have gone through a great deal of anguish at the time of the Cuban missile crisis as he sought to determine the right course of action.

When you meet with adversity as a leader, it is understandable to feel worried. This is a normal human reaction. Nevertheless, it is vital that you overcome this feeling by spurring yourself on and mustering your courage.

95

Don't Use Force Unless Necessary

A leader should always try to win without fighting

ONE OF THE SAYINGS in the *Sun-tzu*, the late Chou classic on the military arts, goes as follows: "As a rule, it is better to save a country than to destroy it. It is better to spare an army than to crush it. To win all one's battles decisively is not necessarily the best result. The best path is to overcome your opponents without eradicating them."

* * *

The *Sun-tzu* advocated winning victory through superior strategy rather than through force of arms. Think about it, and you'll find this a sensible approach. Warfare is a means to an end, not an end in itself. If you can win without fighting, so much the better.

Toyotomi Hideyoshi rose rapidly to power using tactics similar to those espoused in the *Sun-tzu*. In some of his battles, such as the one against Akechi Mitsuhide, he fought like a demon, recklessly expending the lives of his men. His preferred method, however, was to convert enemies into allies by diplomatic means. When forced to fight, he would field an army vastly outnumbering his opponent's and was often able to prompt his enemies to surrender before battle began.

It was because Hideyoshi always tried to win without fighting that he was able to unify the country in such a short time. If he had had to fight each warlord individually, the country would have been thrown into turmoil, even if he managed to win all his battles. Japan could not have recovered from such chaos quickly.

This principle applies equally to present-day business management. When competing with another company, look for a solution that allows both sides to win something.

If you engage in no-holds-barred competition and get the better of your rival by sheer strength, you will both get hurt and society at large will suffer. This route to victory is not acceptable today: you must live and let live, competing in a manner that allows your competitor to prosper while you prosper. Regardless of the approach you take, you cannot truly be called a great leader unless you can win without fighting.

96

The Art of Issuing Orders

A leader must give commands that he expects will be obeyed

AT THE TIME OF the Shimabara Revolt in 1637, the Tokugawa shogunate was led by General Itakura Shigemasa. But Shigemasa's orders were frequently ignored by the Kyushu lords, who resented being under the command of a low-ranking general. In the end, the general died in an ill-advised attack.

His successor was Matsudaira Nobutsuna, known as Wise Izu. Although the leading councilor to the shogun, he was only a minor lord with a small fief. His low status meant that the other lords were as disrespectful of him as they had been of his predecessor.

But Nobutsuna developed a clever plan to counter the intransigence of his fellows. First he decreed that anyone who disobeyed military orders would be brought before the shogunate cabinet and severely punished. Then he persuaded the shogun, Tokugawa Iemitsu, to provide him with a large quantity of paper, embossed with the shogun's hollyhock seal, for writing his military orders. Nobutsuna demanded written acknowledgment of receipt of orders from each daimyo and they soon had no choice but to acknowledge their responsibilities and obey the orders of the new leader. In a short time, discipline was restored.

* * *

Anyone in the position of leader must give orders. But just because an order is given does not necessarily mean it will be carried out. A leader must see to it that his orders are obeyed in the way he intends, otherwise they will be of little effect.

An order is only executed if the recipient is strongly motivated to carry it out. A leader must, therefore, pay attention to his subordinates and consider the most effective way to make his orders count.

Rather than just giving orders, a leader can often get better results by taking a consultative role, involving the subordinate in determining the order. This allows a degree of autonomy, rather than just a response to orders from above, and is usually a better approach.

If, as Nobutsuna found, the subordinate does not respect the leader's authority, such an approach will only make matters worse. Hence he needed to emphasize his own authority, backed up by that of the shogun, which explains the method he used to make his subordinates aware of their responsibilities.

Whatever the circumstances, remember that giving an order is not enough in itself. It is important to present the order in a way that makes the recipient accept responsibility for carrying it out.

97

Setting Goals

It is the leader's job to set the right targets

ON JULY 20, 1969, ASTRONAUTS from the U.S. spacecraft Apollo 11 landed on the moon, taking man's first steps on another planet. Just a few short years before, such an event seemed impossible. The dream became reality through the labors of a vast number of scientists and support personnel.

The ambitious Apollo moonshot program began with the declaration by President John F. Kennedy in 1961 that America would put a man on the moon by the end of the decade. By setting the target of a manned moon landing, Kennedy focussed the intellect and abilities of a large number of people, leading to the success represented by the Apollo 11 mission. It was an achievement of truly historic significance.

*   *   *

An important function of a leader is to set goals. Even without specialized knowledge of a subject, he must still be able to identify the target.

Kennedy didn't need to be a scientist to set the goal of a moon landing but he had to be a leader. It is the leader's responsibility to understand what sort of objectives can be attained and set the goals accordingly. He can, and should, seek the advice of those with the requisite technical expertise, but the final decision will be his.

Once the target has been set, all manner of people will contribute their talent and expertise toward achieving it. When people's efforts are focussed in this way, even a project as momentous and daunting as a moon landing becomes possible. Without a target, however, a team cannot function effectively, regardless of the talent at its disposal.

Thus a leader must set, one after the other, goals that he judges to be appropriate to the circumstances on the basis of his experience and managerial vision. It is only a slight exaggeration to say that if he can do this well he need not do anything else.

98

Doing It Your Way

A leader will not succeed unless he uses his own unique abilities

GUANG WU DI, WHO laid the foundations of the Later Han dynasty, subdued Longxi in the process of unifying China and then faced resistance from the neighboring district of Shu. Proclaimed the emperor, "Human beings are never satisfied. Today I gained Longxi, but now I want to be ruler of Shu." Shortly afterwards he mobilized his troops, then successfully took Shu.

Two hundred years later during the period of the Three Kingdoms, Cao Cao of Wei moved his troops into Longxi. At that point, his men urged him to take Shu as well, but Cao Cao quelled them, saying, "I am not Guang Wu Di. I have already taken Longxi; why should I want Shu also?"

* * *

Both Guang Wu Di and Cao Cao were great heroes. One said "I have Longxi and now I want Shu," while the other said, "Now I have Longxi, why should I want Shu?" Both were right, because both based their decisions on the circumstances, which were different in each case.

Some years ago, Yamaoka Sohachi's best-seller about Tokugawa Ieyasu sparked an Ieyasu boom in Japan. Ieyasu was one of the most outstanding leaders in Japan's history, whose life story holds many lessons for us. Merely emulating his actions, however, is no guarantee of success. Ieyasu's approach succeeded because he was Ieyasu; anyone trying to imitate him will probably fail. Rather than imitate other leaders slavishly, you should take hints from their approach and adapt the lessons you learn from their experience to your own circumstances.

Everyone has his own way of doing things; no two people are exactly alike. Every leader must use his own unique talents to the full and do things in his own fashion.

In this sense, I consider Cao Cao the greater hero. Knowing the historical facts, he recognized that he was a different kind of man in a different situation and was able to disregard Guang Wu Di's precedent.

99

Be Brave

A leader needs courage drawn from virtue not from foolhardiness

CONFUCIUS, TALKING ONE DAY with his followers, praised his disciple Yan Hui very highly. On hearing this, Zi Lu, a disciple who excelled in military prowess, asked, "Master, if you had to muster an army to fight, who would you choose?" Behind his question was the implication that the weaker Yan Hui would be of no use and that Confucius should choose someone strong and brave—Zi Lu, for example.

Confucius replied, "I would not choose someone rash enough to take on a tiger barehanded, wade through a deep river, or disregard my orders in an emergency. It would have to be someone who would plan carefully and act prudently." His reply put Zi Lu in his place.

*   *   *

Confucius is not denying the importance of courage. On another occasion, he is said to have remarked, "Every virtuous man is a courageous man." Virtue means knowing the path to follow, which leads to the bravery to follow that path. The courage simply to strike out blindly is foolhardy and not really courage at all.

I myself learned this through a similar experience. A few years after I set up my business, a rival company started heavily undercutting my prices. Being young, I thought to myself, "Very well, if that's the way they want it, they've got a price war on their hands. I won't let them get the better of me."

I consulted a priest about the matter. "If you were on your own," he said, "it wouldn't matter how rashly you acted. But since you have a large number of employees, all of whom have families, it would be foolhardy to try to outdo your rival. A boss must not get carried away and start acting recklessly."

Hearing this, I had second thoughts, and did what I knew to be right—I refrained from getting caught up in a price war. In the long run, this won me the trust of my customers and built the foundations of my later success.

A leader needs to be courageous, not mere recklessness or foolhardy. He must always ask himself what is right and have the courage to do what needs to be done, however many people disagree with him.

100

Keep Your Wits About You

A leader must be vigilant at all times

WHEN KATO KIYOMASA WAS fighting in Korea, he received a summons from Toyotomi Hideyoshi. On his way back from the battlezone, he was received by his friend, Commander Toda Takamasa, some distance behind the Japanese front line.

No Korean troops were around and the enemy seemed to have been completely subdued. Takamasa and his retainers came to meet Kato Kiyomasa in civilian clothing, but Kiyomasa's troops were in full battledress, and Kiyomasa was carrying a survival kit containing rice, miso, and some silver coins when he entered the castle.

Somewhat disgruntled, Takamasa said, "There are no enemy troops about, so why are you dressed in full uniform?" To which Kiyomasa replied, "It is true that there is no immediate danger, but it is also true that many disasters arise through carelessness. If we become careless in the enemy's absence and relax our guard, then a sudden change in the situation will mean that all our military gains to date will be lost. Even if this does not happen, the men will become sloppy. If the leader lets up even slightly, the men will do the same and become careless. To prevent this, I never cut any corners, as you can see." Takamasa was deeply impressed.

* * *

People generally prefer the easy option. In periods of extended peace, they take tranquility for granted and are only jogged out of their complacency when an emergency arises. But as noted earlier in this volume, there is an old proverb that reads, "Forget not war in times of peace."

Everyone would prefer peace to continue indefinitely, but the world is always changing, and we never know what is ahead. So even when all is quiet and things are going well, we should still be prepared for trouble and upheaval. As well as preparing ourselves mentally, we must also take concrete action; neither the spiritual nor physical aspects should be neglected.

This is very important for any individual, and even more important for leaders like Kato Kiyomasa. Once a leader becomes soft, orders to his subordinates to remain vigilant will have little effect.

101

Beyond Reason

**A leader must sometimes
acknowledge intuitions which
transcend ordinary logic**

DURING THE WARRING STATES period in China there lived
a great general by the name of Zhao She in the kingdom of Zhao. It happened that the neighboring Qin
army invaded part of Zhao and completely surrounded
the area. The king of Zhao asked his generals whether
the area could be restored to the kingdom. All but one
replied that this was very unlikely, as the district was far
away and on high ground. Zhao She alone responded
differently, "The road is long and steep," he said "and
if we fight the enemy there we shall be like two rats
fighting in a hole: the braver one will win." The king
sent Zhao She to the disputed area, where he defeated
the Qin army.

* * *

"Reason beyond reason" goes the saying. In theory, one plus one should always make two, but this is not necessarily true in practice. Sometimes the answer may be ten, sometimes it may be a minus figure. Simple logic is not enough.

Reason beyond reason is logic that happens on a higher plane working in a way we cannot discern and can only accept.

In the above incident, the other generals decided that the distance and position of the lost territory meant that it could not be recaptured. They acted logically. It required a grasp of reason beyond reason to perceive that the logical failure they saw could turn out to be a success in practice.

Zhao She had a son, Zhao Kuo, who studied military tactics. One day, when father and son were discussing military matters, Zhao She found himself unable to answer an argument put forward by his son, but still he would not concede the point. When his wife asked him the reason for this, he replied, "Warfare is a matter of life and death. Zhao Kuo thinks it is a simple matter of logic. If he ever becomes a general, this country will be ruined."

Several years after Zhao She died, the kingdom of Zhao once again faced the Qin army, this time with Zhao Kuo leading the army. Following his own logic he made an all-out attack on the enemy's military command and was soundly defeated, losing several hundred thousand soldiers. The kingdom of Zhao was greatly diminished as a result.

Educated people tend to see things logically and become so preoccupied that they discount the reason that transcends reason. Of course, education and logic are important, but a leader must not let them blind him to recognition of a higher form of reasoning.

102

Another Look at Modesty and Humility

A true leader is not burdened with conceit

IN THIS BOOK, I have presented anecdotes about historical figures to illustrate the qualities a good leader needs. Admirable as these historical figures may be, I know that there are leaders today in many fields who are every bit as good. Indeed, among the leaders I have been fortunate enough to meet, several have been outstanding and all have achieved great things while being extremely likeable as people.

I do not know in detail how these people think and act in their daily capacity as leaders. But I gather from our conversations that their conduct closely mirrors the various precepts described in this book. The thing that struck me about all these leaders was their modesty and humility. I believe that this quality is shared by all the great contemporary leaders I have met.

I can think of people who managed to achieve steady growth for their organizations in the midst of an economic slump. None of them was the least bit conceited. One even said, "I'm grateful, but it seems too good to be true and that worries me!" This leader then sought my advice about setting up a think tank.

On another occasion, I went to visit a top-level leader and found my host waiting for me in the foyer a good ten minutes before our appointment. The welcome I received was so deferential that I was embarrassed. Such leaders show not the slightest trace of arrogance.

I conclude that although each one of these people was the top leader of their company or organization, they were also the most modest and humble members in it. Since they also dealt with people outside the company in this modest manner, they were on good terms with everyone and acted as a natural magnet. I believe that this is the secret of their success.

The subjects of modesty and humility were discussed earlier in this book, but recent experiences have again brought home to me the importance of these qualities in a leader. Hence I bring them to your attention again in my concluding chapter.

Index
of
Personal Names

Adenauer, Konrad (1876–1967) 6
Akechi Mitsuharu (1537–82) 134
Akechi Mitsuhide (1526–82) 38,
  108, 148, 178, 181, 191
Ando Naotsugu (1544–1635) 60
Archimedes (287–212 B.C.) 31, 54
Asai Nagamasa (1545–73) 112

Baba Nobufusa (1515–75) 160

Cao Cao (155–220) 168, 196
Carnegie, Andrew (1835–1915)
  142
Chiang Kai-shek (1887–1975) 140
Chiba Hirotsune (?–1183) 46
Clark, William (1826–86) 52
Confucius (552–479 B.C.) 53, 67,
  70, 111, 138, 172, 184, 198

Date Masamune (1567–1636)
  158
Doi Toshikatsu (1573–1644) 60
Duke Huan (?–643 B.C.) 180

Edison, Thomas (1874–1931) 146
Eisenhower, Dwight (1890–1969)
  6

Fan Zeng (?–204 B.C.) 88, 167
Fu Cha (?–473 B.C.) 36

Fukushima Masanori (1561–1624)
  42
Fukuzawa Yukichi (1835–1901)
  143, 150

Gou Jian (?–465 B.C.) 36
Guan Zhong (?–645 B.C.) 154, 180
Guang Wu Di (6B.C.–A.D.57)
  90, 196

Han Xin (?–197 B.C.) 166
He Lu (?–492 B.C.) 36
Heraclitus (ca.540–ca.470 B.C.)
  173
Hojo Ujimasa (1538–90) 128
Hojo Ujiyasu (1515–71) 128
Honda Masazumi (1565–1637) 58
Hori Hidemasa (1553–90) 20, 26,
  92
Hoshina Masayuki (1611–72) 40,
  78

Iida Kakubei (?–1632) 182
Ikeda Mitsumasa (1609–82) 2, 114
Imagawa Yoshimoto (1519–60)
  32, 73, 102
Ishida Mitsunari (1560–1600) 58,
  186
Itakura Katsushige (1545–1624)
  114

Ito Hirobumi (1841–1909) 165
Iwakura Tomomi (1825–83) 100
Iwasaki Yataro (1834–85) 76

Ji Bu (fl. 3rd cent. B.C.) 86
Jiang Jie-shi 140
  (*See* Chiang Kai-shek)

Kanmu Emperor (737–806) 39
Kato Kiyomasa (1562–1611) 94,
  182, 200
Katsu Kaishu (1823–99) 10, 120,
  174
Kennedy, John F. (1917–63) 122,
  189, 194
Khrushchev, Nikita (1894–1971)
  122
Kido Takayoshi (1833–77) 62
Kinoshita Tokichiro 44 (*See*
  Toyotomi Hideyoshi)
Kitsukawa Motoharu (1530–86)
Kobayakawa Takakage (1533–97)
  148
Komura Jutaro (1855–1911) 10
Kosaka Masanobu (1527–78) 160
Kuroda Yoshitaka (1546–1604) 98
Kuroki Tametomo (1844–1923) 30

Lincoln, Abraham (1809–65) 99
Liu Bei (161–223) 168,170
Liu Bang (247-195 B.C.) 86, 88,
  166

Maeda Toshiie (1538–99) 42, 118
Mao Zedong (1893–1976) 64, 117,
  143
Ma Su (190–228) 80
Matsudaira Nobutsuna (1596–
  1662) 192
Matsudaira Sadanobu (1758–1829)
  12
Matsunaga Hisahide (1510–77)
  135
Meiji, Emperor (1852–1912) 126

Minamoto Noriyori (?–1193) 116
Minamoto Yoritomo (1147–99)
  46, 59, 116
Minamoto Yoshitsune (1159–89)
  116
Miyamoto Musashi (1584–1645)
  56
Mori family 96, 109, 148, 178, 189
Mo Zi (fl. 6th cent. B.C.) 22

Napoleon, Bonaparte I (1769–
  1821) 176
Newton, Sir Isaac (1643–1727) 31
Nichiren, Saint (1222–82) 53, 68
Nintoku, (fl. 5th cent.) Emperor
  79
Nitobe Inazo (1862–1933) 52

Oda Nobunaga (1534–82) 32, 38,
  43, 44, 72, 102, 104, 109, 112,
  148, 178, 181
Onda Moku (1717–62) 14
Omura Masujiro (1824–69) 4, 63
Ooka Tadasuke (1677–1751) 130

Perry, Commodore Matthew
  (1794–1858) 164

Saicho (767–822) 39
Saigo Takamori (1827–77) 62,
  120, 174, 189
Sakuma Morimasa (1554–83) 108
Sanada Yukihiro (1740–1815) 14
Sasaki Shotei 18
Sassa Narimasa (?–1588) 118
Sato Shosuke (1856–1939) 52
Shang Yang (?–338 B.C.) 48
Shibata, Katsuie (1522–83) 18,
  108
Shimazu Nariakira (1809–58) 174
Shimazu Yoshihisa (1533–1611)
Shimazu Muneharu (1537–82) 96
Shinran, Saint (1173–1262) 28
Shotoku, Prince (574–622) 24

Sima Zhongda (179–251) 84
Socrates (469?–399 B.C.) 110
Su Qin (?–317 B.C.) 156
Sun Quan (182–252) 168

Takasugi Shinsaku (1839–67) 144
Takeda Katsuyori (1546–82) 72, 104
Takeda Shingen (1521–73) 8, 72, 82, 104, 132, 160
Tang, (fl. 16th cent. B.C.) King 172
Toda Takamasa (?–?) 200
Todo Takatora (1556–1630) 16
Tokugawa Iemitsu (1604–51) 193
Tokugawa Ieyasu (1542–1616) 12, 16, 20, 27, 43, 58, 60, 72, 85, 94, 104, 130, 132, 197
Tokugawa Mitsukuni (1628–1700) 162
Tokugawa Tsunayoshi (1646–1709)
Tokugawa Yorifusa (1603–61) 162
Tokugawa Yoshimune (1684–1751) 130
Tokugawa Yoshinobu (1837–1913) 75
Toyotomi Hideyori (1593–1615) 94
Toyotomi Hideyoshi (1536–98) 16, 20, 43, 45, 66, 94, 96, 98, 108, 132, 134, 148, 152, 158, 181, 186, 191, 200 (See Kinoshita Tokichiro)

Uchimura Kanzo (1861–1930) 52
Uesugi Harunori (1751–1822) 124
Uesugi Kenshin (1530–78) 8
Umewaka Minoru (1828–1909) 34

Wang Mi (fl. 2nd cent.) 50
Watanabe Satoru (1562–1640) 16

Yamagata Aritomo (1838–1922) 165
Yamagata Masakage (?–1575) 160
Yamanaka Shikanosuke (1544?–78) 188
Yamaoka Sohachi (1907–78) 197
Yamashina Takigoro (1807?–76) 34
Yan Hui (514–483 B.C.) 198
Yang Zhen (?–124) 50
Yao, (legendary) Emperor 106
Yoshida Shoin (1830–59) 164

Xiao He (?–193 B.C.) 167
Xiang Yu (?–202 B.C.) 86, 88, 167

Zeng Shen (fl. 5th cent. B.C.) 70
Zhang Liang (?–168 B.C.) 99, 167
Zhao Kuo (fl. 3rd cent. B.C.) 203
Zhao She (fl. 3rd cent. B.C.) 202
Zhou Enlai (1898–1976) 117
Zhuge Liang (181–234) 80, 84, 140, 168, 170
Zi Jian (fl. 5th cent. B.C.) 184
Zi Lu (543 B.C.–?) 198

Chronology
of
Japanese History

Jomon	ca. 7500 B.C.–ca. 300 B.C.
Yayoi	ca. 300 B.C.–ca. A.D. 300
Kofun	ca. A.D. 300–ca. 500
Asuka and Hakuho	552– 710
Nara	710– 794
Heian	794–1185
Kamakura	1185–1333
Muromachi	1338–1568
Civil War (Sengoku)	1573–1603
Edo (Tokugawa)	1603–1868
Modern	1868–present
Meiji	1868–1912
Taisho	1912–1926
Showa	1926–1989
Heisei	1989–present